Dear Church
Letters from a Disillusioned Generation

Dear Church

Letters from a Disillusioned Generation

Sarah Cunningham

ZONDERVAN®

GRAND RAPIDS, MICHIGAN 49530 USA

ZONDERVAN.COM/
AUTHORTRACKER

ZONDERVAN®

Dear Church
Copyright © 2006 by Sarah Raymond Cunningham

Requests for information should be addressed to:
Zondervan, *Grand Rapids, Michigan 49530*

Library of Congress Cataloging-in-Publication Data

Cunningham, Sarah.
    Dear church : letters from a disillusioned generation / Sarah Cunningham.
      p. cm.
    Includes bibliographical references.
    ISBN-10: 0-310-26958-X
    ISBN-13: 978-0-310-26958-8
    1. Church controversies. 2. Generation X—Religious life.
    3. Generation Y—Religious life. I. Title.
    BV652.9.C86 2006
    262—dc22
2005037177

Scripture quotations, unless otherwise indicated, are taken from the *Holy Bible, Today's New International Version*™. TNIV®. Copyright © 2001 by International Bible Society. Used by permission of Zondervan. All rights reserved.

Scripture quotations marked NIV are taken from the *Holy Bible: New International Version*®. NIV®. Copyright © 1973, 1978, 1984 by International Bible Society. Used by permission of Zondervan. All rights reserved.

Scripture quotations marked KJV are taken from the King James Version of the Bible.

The website addresses recommended throughout this book are offered as a resource to you. These websites are not intended in any way to be or imply an endorsement on the part of Zondervan, nor do we vouch for their content for the life of this book.

Interior design by Michelle Espinoza

Printed in the United States of America

06 07 08 09 10 11 12 • 18 17 16 15 14 13 12 11 10 9 8 7 6 5 4 3 2

To my church...
My parents, Harold and Elizabeth Raymond,
who led the first Christian community I ever belonged to: my family.

My brothers, David and John,
who model the love of spiritual siblings while
tormenting me like genetic ones.

My coconspirators, Jennie and Bethany,
who continue to believe we can change the world.

The people of Cornerstone and Westwinds,
who helped me fall in love with the local church,

and

my pastor and friend, Ron Martoia,
who continually inspires me to love the global one.

And most of all, my husband, Chuck,
who partners with me in living and being church to our local world.

I am grateful to Jesus, the head of the church,
for teaming me with people like these.

Contents

This Is Important

Dear Readers,

I used to believe that the church was the most powerful source of hope on the planet. That is, until I got old enough to notice its defects.

Once in adult land, I quickly stumbled upon a list of religious flaws and a side of the church that was far from hopeful.

Unfortunately, I am not the only one who lost some admiration for the church along the way. Many of my fellow twenty-somethings ended up less than impressed with the church as well. And sadly, as my peers dropped out of local congregations, they were promptly welcomed into a multigenerational group of ex–church attenders.

Apparently, disillusionment has been sidetracking the church attenders of our world for some time.

Granted, the disillusioned don't always ditch the church scene altogether. Some of the people in the pews are just as disgruntled as those playing hooky. Almost everyone seems to have a story to tell about some painful encounter with the church.

So whether you are disgruntled with the church right this minute or whether you're just concerned about a friend who is jaded by organizational Christianity, I invite you to correspond with me and my generation about your experiences.

Do I think a simple exchange of letters can eliminate our frustrations altogether? No. I suspect that as long as we have ideals, we will have disillusionment.

I hope, though, that as long as we have disillusionment, we will fight it together.

Headed toward fullness,
Sarah

Read This First

Dear Church,

You're probably wondering who I am and why I suddenly decided to write you.

I don't blame you for being curious. Or even a little suspicious.

But, if you read a little further, I don't think I'll remain a stranger long. In fact, you may discover that you already know me.

I have a familiar face. Or at least I used to.

I am the Christian twentysomething.

As of late, sources suggest that my relationship with you, Church, is in critical condition.

But these letters aren't just about me. Nor does their content belong exclusively to my generation.

As the title *Dear Church* suggests, these letters are for the *entire* church. And I don't just mean those who currently attend a local church building. Perhaps even more so, these letters are addressed to those who have crossed paths with the church but have chosen not to attend weekly worship services.

To simplify things, then, I have chosen to address the church generically. Keep in mind, though, that when I refer to my reader as the "Church," I am not addressing a steepled building nor am I addressing any one individual or local congregation. Rather, I am referencing the collective — all of us seeking a community that lives out the teachings of Christ.

While everyone, then, is welcome to read this correspondence, it is especially directed to those who:

1. Have been or are currently disillusioned with organized Christianity, or
2. Are leaders in local churches or organizations.

I chose these two groups for slightly different reasons, of course. If you are disillusioned, for instance, I invite you to join me in exploring the experiences that jaded you toward the church. I hope you will be inspired to sift through the feelings surrounding your frustrations, that you will identify any bitterness that can be released, and that you will gain some skills and perspective for dealing with future disappointments. I hope you will join me in opening the communication lines that will earn space for new ideas and priorities in the church of tomorrow. And I hope that together we can recover ways to breathe new life into the faith systems of the future.

If you are a church leader, I hope you will benefit from such a raw telling of how disillusionment has affected me and some in my generation. I hope you will hear things that people might be hesitant to say to you in person. And I hope that you will be encouraged to help my peers and others examine their disillusionment so they can experience more of the fullness that comes with living Christ's ideals.

And while many examples are drawn from my life and the lives of my twentysomething peers, you don't have to worry if you no longer qualify as a "twentysomething." Regardless of age, I am pretty sure some of these words might strike you as familiar. You may have even spoken them yourself at one time or another.

Odds are, you once stood in our idealistic Skechers and believed, like my generation, that the church could change the world. And, on many occasions, you struggled and still struggle — just as we do — against the idea that it cannot.

Perhaps, then, you know how to proceed from this stage that some of my generation find themselves in. Perhaps you can help us recover what we have lost. And perhaps, somewhere along the way, you will be reminded of something you misplaced as well.

As you can imagine, it is a bit tricky to address the entire church in a single shot. I cannot, for example, explain my positions on every topic that relates to the church at large. I cannot communicate everything I would like you to know about myself.

Although I can't anticipate or disclaim myself from every instance in which one particular group might critique or misread me, I hope you pick up on one crucial observation: I have not given up.

True, my church history has included some disappointing events. And yes, I have been and continue to be frustrated when Christian religious systems seem to fall short of the community God intended his followers to experience. However, my belief in the ideal of church—in God's design for those who align themselves with him—is uncompromised. And my sense of hope, a hope that is sourced in the Creator and his Son, is unquestionably intact.

Thus, despite the tensions and letdowns along my spiritual journey, there is no tension I'd rather engage; no cause I'd rather expend my energy on. More than anything else on the planet, I want my world to shift their allegiance to Christ and to live in the fullness God intended for them.

I believe, without question, that what lies on the other side of disillusionment is a kind of wholeness, peace, and purpose that makes every struggle worthwhile. And even in those moments when disillusionment seems like it will never end, I am convinced that God is present.

In forcing myself to bring my own concerns and the resulting learnings to expression, I have had to dig for the maturity and wisdom to face my own questions, examine my own flaws, and review my own position before God and others. This has been a priceless journey for me, and as a result, it is a journey I wish on every one of you.

Along these lines, I am hoping you will do more than just read my letters. I am hoping you will respond to them. To invite you to participate in this correspondence, I've included discussion questions that you can use for personal journaling or to spur group conversation. There is also a website, *www.dearchurch.com*, where you can post your own letters to the church.

part 1

Introducing the Twentysomethings

Not Fine

Dear Church,

I have wanted to write you for years, but I was never exactly sure what to say. Writing letters used to be so simple. My early attempts all started the same way: *Dear So and So, How are you?*

The second sentence was equally gripping: *I am fine.* Even at five years old, I knew that people are supposed to say they are fine. Not to mention that printing "I am spectacular" or "I am distressed" would have taken forever on that red-and-black-lined kindergarten paper.

If only correspondence were still five-year-old simple.

Well, when in doubt, go with what you know, right?

Dear Church, how the heck are you?

Learned anything lately? Surviving all your international projects? On the brink of any crazy ideas?

I hope, of course, that you and yours are well.

Me? Well, I'm not exactly basking in the spiritual high life. Unlike my kindergarten self, I am not always fine these days. And unfortunately, it's not just me, Church. Many of my peers seem to be calling in sick as well.

You may have read, or at least heard, the statistics on my generation's church attendance. If not, let's just say that you might want to think about adding truancy officers to your local church staffs.

George Barna, president of the Barna Group, compiled research from surveys of 2,660 twentysomethings and found that "Americans in their twenties are significantly less likely than any other age group to attend church services, to donate to churches, to be absolutely committed to Christianity, to read the Bible, or to serve as a volunteer or lay leader in churches."[1]

Barna, of course, is not the only one noticing my generation's shift away from the institutional church. We haven't been nominated for the perfect attendance trophy in *anyone's* award ceremony. Well-known church consultant Bill Easum warns of even wider attendance losses. He points out that "the vast majority of the population under 40 years of age is unchurched."[2]

Not only are the twentysomethings' pews getting cold, so is our commitment to religion in general. As a 2004 Gallup poll reports, "Younger Americans are more likely than those who are older to claim no religion."[3]

My generation's dwindling relationship with the church and its faith systems also have captured the attention of Christian authors. In 2002, Robert Webber's *Younger Evangelicals* put the spotlight on twentysomething or young-in-spirit adults who "freely acknowledge that they differ with the pragmatist's approach to ministry."[4]

Dave Tomlinson, author of *The Post-Evangelical*, also underlined changing faith trends among younger-variety Christians. According to him, this group has "difficulty reconciling what they see and experience in evangelicalism with their own values, theological reflection and intuition."[5]

To tactfully state the obvious, many twentysomethings are disillusioned with you, Church.

I am no exception.

Born a PK (read: Pastor's Kid, not Promise Keeper), I logged hundreds of hours in the pews before I ever learned to pronounce the word *church*.

While some parents struggled to get their kids to take ownership in the local church, I presented a different challenge. Not only did I take ownership in our local church's mission, I *literally* seemed to think I *owned* the building. I would have bet my offering that my signature was on the church deed, scribbled with the same visitor pen I used to play tic-tac-toe on the back of bulletins.

In fact, I probably still owe a few apologies to the many well-meaning adults who occasionally reminded me not to run in the church hallways. As I sped by, unaffected by their warnings, I would flash them the obviously-you-don't-realize-who-you're-talking-to look. *These are MY hallways.*

As a pastor's kid, I took my role in the local church very seriously. Among a long list of other self-appointed responsibilities, I was in charge of flashing my dad a handwritten "It's 12:05!" sign when a particularly long sermon didn't seem to be coming in for a landing.

In short, my childhood was an eighteen-year course on Christian leadership. And while I like to joke about having front-row seats to seven days of sermons a week, I would not trade my initiation to the church for anything.

By the time I graduated from high school, I was on track to carry out Christ's mission with atypical intensity. I immediately gravitated toward Spring Arbor University, a Christian college in south-central Michigan that provided the perfect context for experimenting with my evolving ministry ideas. I doubt anyone was surprised four years later when, before I even received my degree, I launched my adult career as a full-time staffer at a local church.

And not just any local church. Westwinds, my first place of employment, was hands-down the most compelling context I'd ever seen the word *church* attached to. The attenders were passionate, the services were creative, the staff was driven. As a result of being teamed with this congregation, my adult years seemed to pick up right where my childhood left off: I was living, breathing, and bleeding church and having the time of my life doing it.

The more time I invested in local church, the more I believed — I mean *really seriously believed* — the premise that "the church is the hope of the world."

Of course, as the veterans among you can probably guess, my lifetime of church-related euphoria did not always exist unchallenged. During certain phases of my journey, Church, you seemed to lose a little bit of your hopeful shine.

Throughout my childhood, and at important junctures in my adulthood, I began to pick up that not everyone's encounters with the church were as positive as mine. Not everyone, as it turned out, got the full-blown PK package: hugs in the church foyer, cookies at Christmas, or invitations to play at house after house.

Slowly, I grew concerned that my experience with church was not necessarily the norm. Several months before taking my first church staff position, I enrolled in an additional learning track at Spring Arbor University. My urban studies minor, conducted under the supervision of sociology professor Paul Nemecek, allowed me to craft an independent study that examined how local churches interacted with diverse people groups in our city.

Block after block, I surveyed citizens of our town. More often than not, these interviews produced thought-provoking stories.

The comments from a woman working in connection with the local justice department summarized the feelings of many. "What do you think churches could do to improve their relationship with the local community?" I asked.

"Churches?" she repeated, almost as if she thought she might have heard me wrong.

I nodded and repeated the question.

"I don't see anything that churches could do." She wasn't being mean, but rather to-the-point. "We've already got tons of churches. Look around. There's a church on every corner. I bet you could count nine or ten within three blocks of here," she reminded me. "And nothing has changed, has it? Did you know that three or four of these churches have been here since the town was on the map? But some of the social issues just keep getting worse and worse."

She paused for me to write things down. "People don't have enough job training or employment opportunities. Drunks wander the streets. The same homeless people have been circling in and out of the shelters for the last fifteen years. Kids don't have anything to do to keep them out of trouble. Meanwhile, the churches keep right on existing, holding their services every Sunday. And it never changes anything. It seems pretty obvious to me that churches are not the answer."

Day after day I turned up similar impressions—sometimes so many that I ended up crying the five-mile drive back to campus. The church that many of these people perceived was not the church I wanted to represent.

After all those years running up and down your halls, weaving in and out of adult legs in your lobby, playing freeze tag on your lawn, and chilling with your people, I was extremely offended on your behalf, Church.

As much as I loved you, Church, in those moments, I was very disappointed in you. Almost—dare I say it—embarrassed to be a part of you. Slowly, as my research continued, I began to entertain the idea of investing my energies elsewhere, in an organization outside of the church.

A couple years prior, I would never have voiced such things out loud. Admitting that "sometimes I don't want to be part of the church" would have been like saying "I think I'll become a Nazi" in some church circles.

On the contrary, Church, if someone pointed out a chink in your shiny silver armor, I would rush forward and create some clever diversion. As the audience watched me dance and sing and tell jokes, their attention would be drawn away from the church's flaws long enough for the stagehands to rush in and apply some cover-up to your image.

But by the time I finished my independent study, I was no longer willing to pretend that the church was ten for ten in dispensing hope.

I, of course, am not alone in my critiques of the church-equals-hope equation.

While I don't want anyone to engrave my generation's spiritual gravestones just yet, I must admit that the feedback I get from many of my contemporaries—even Christian ones—is consistent with the responses generated by my informal survey.

As I meet with a small group of peers each week, our local conversation is consistent with the national, some say international, trend. The questions that have consumed the church's attention are no longer center topics in our circles. Gone are the days when we intensely debated the literal interpretation of the Creation narrative. We desperately want our peers to acknowledge God as Creator, but we're not losing sleep over whether they think those seven days were twenty-four hours long or longer.

We're not captivated by the banter over whether believers are predestined or whether they accept Christ through free choice. Since we're already experiencing a relationship with God, we figure we'll just wait for the postlife course, How It All Really Worked 101, to nail down the details.

And, please, don't send us a rerelease of *88 Reasons Why the Rapture Is in 1988* (an actual book released in, you guessed it, 1988).[6] We really don't mind whether God raptures us pre- or posttrib. The point is Jesus is coming back, right?

Don't get us wrong, Church. We value these theological questions. We really do. And we understand, for instance, that we cannot sacrifice literal interpretation of one chapter without opening the door for reinterpreting all chapters.

Frankly, we admire thinkers within the church for wrestling their own generation's questions to the ground. However, we must note: their hang-ups are not our hang-ups. We twentysomething Christians can't focus too much energy on analyzing intricate church doctrines because, quite honestly, our peers aren't even close enough to the church to know what the doctrines in question are.

Unlike some previous generations, our peers are not delaying their salvation based on unresolved questions about Creationism.

More times than not, they are delaying their salvation based on unresolved questions, anger, or misperceptions about the church itself.

Sadly, no matter where I am in the United States, I half expect twentysomethings to voice some sort of irritation when the word *church* is mentioned. (Granted, this probably has as much to do with our outspokenness as it does with any flaws on the church's part.)

Just the other day I was talking with a local coffee shop regular when, completely unprovoked by me, he began venting about his experiences with the Christian church. A twenty-seven-year-old with a Jewish background, he offered a quick "I hope you're not a Christian or anything because I wouldn't want to offend you" disclaimer before listing off a number of offensive encounters he has had with organized Christianity.

"It appears I don't have the truth." He smirked, his voice thick with bitterness. "As soon as church people figure out I'm Jewish, they immediately rule out my credibility. Nothing I can say could possibly be legitimate or worthy of discussing because their tunnel vision is focused on one thing and one thing alone: we need to get this guy to see the error of his ways.

"To tell you the truth, I'm not even that hung up on Judaism," he admitted, lowering his voice as if he didn't want any Christians to hear him. Laughing, he exhaled smoke into the air. "It's just the best thing I've got thus far. If anyone with a little courtesy could show me differently, I'd be all ears. Until then, I've got no use for Christians."

A day later, I got a package from a twenty-six-year-old friend with whom I took a class while spending a semester in Chicago. Although we hadn't talked in several years, I sent him a copy of these letters. He took them along on a plane ride and ended up penning me a lengthy response.

On one page, he wrote: "My question is: Why should I stay in church? Why should I try to go through the disillusionment? What does the church offer that you can't get anywhere else?"

As I tried to capture such real-life reflections in these letters, I sought even wider feedback by emailing my letters-in-progress to friends and numerous online acquaintances. Despite my familiarity with twentysomethings' opinionated tendencies, the number and nature of responses I got in return caught me completely off guard.

Not only were their replies usually immediate—sometimes shooting back to me in minutes and almost always within twenty-four hours—they were often incredibly intense. One person reported that she was so disheartened with her current church situation that she clocked out of work and took the morning off to read my letters. Another told me that he readily agreed with some of my perceptions, but asked not to let anyone at his church know that he had talked to me—lest someone see him as subversive and give him the axe. Several others sent email replies that spilled into pages and pages of feedback—a few of which were more lengthy than the letters themselves!

I even got emails from friends of the people I corresponded with, telling me, "I hope you don't mind that I wrote you, but my friend told me about your project and I am really interested in the topic." And almost without fail, each response included firsthand stories of his or her own disillusioning experiences.

Rick, an online acquaintance, wrote: "I think much of what you say resonates with me but frankly I feel a bit excluded in that I hardly qualify, at the age of forty-five, as one of the disillusioned twentysomethings. So I can't help but wonder if there's a way to say what you're saying but not limit your demographics to those twenty years younger.... Bottom line is, I encourage you to go forward but to also consider including the disillusioned who are a tad older. We're out there."

Rick's reaction to the material in these letters wouldn't shock researchers. Observers have long been speculating that my generation can, in some ways, be considered an extension of the generation before them.[7]

Internationals, it seems, also are ready and willing to get in on the conversation. Fredrik, a Swede who has also written on our generation's disconnect from the church, wrote, "I think [disillusionment] is also something very typical for our generation. At least speaking for myself, I'm really tired of the pulpit-pew congregation style because it doesn't transform lives in the same way as one-to-one communication does."*

Given the variety of responses from twentysomethings and other age groups in America and abroad, I would be hard-pressed to capture all their reflections in one series of letters. However, I do think it is possible to pinpoint a few issues that consistently surface as my peers poke and prod at the church's claim to be "the hope of the world."

First, many twentysomethings doubt the church's claim to be inclusive. In fact, many of them think the church is exclusive to a fault. Second, some balk at infractions that seem to undermine "authenticity" in how the church presents itself. Finally, some question whether attending a local church has anything to do with a person's faith. They wonder if sitting in a sanctuary once a week is a valid marker of transformation or spiritual growth.

As you can probably guess, living as a Christian in a society that is skeptical about the church leads to some serious soul searching. Should my generation continue to invest in local churches that don't connect with us and with our peers? Can we maintain unity with the previous generation's churches without sacrificing the best opportunities to influence our generation?

These questions arise as my friends and I read Philippians (see 2:1–2, NIV). We clearly hear Paul's call for unity in the church, but we wonder what exactly he meant by "make my joy complete by being *like-minded, having the same love, being one in spirit and purpose.*"

*Fredrik Hellström is one of a handful of twentysomethings outside of America who provided feedback and insight for these letters. Those who read Swedish can check out his article at *http://crossnet.se/index.phtml?id=469*. English speakers can find out more about him at: *http://nordicinfluence.crossnet.se/index.php?p=24*.

"Does that mean we're stuck where we are? Trapped being *unified* with the same local church as long as we live in this area?" someone asks.

The rest of us shrug, hoping church will never be a synonym for life imprisonment.

"But if your church doesn't actively seek a relationship with *all* people, don't you think you are justified in trying to find a church that will?" another counters.

"Or do you think we're supposed to stick with the church and help them reach the people they are missing?"

Other times, we think we spot loopholes in Paul's writings.

"Wait, I've got it. Technically, can't we be unified with a church *in spirit and purpose* without actually physically attending it?"

"Or, can we start our own church and just be unified with ourselves?" another person says with a laugh.

"But if we live by that rule, won't our own kids one day abandon us to start their own church?"

"Would it be such a bad thing if they did?"

(By the way, we decide it would be. We like intergenerational church.)

We know we are not the first generation to ask these questions, Church. But the church's history—as evidenced in the Reformation, the Great Awakening, and the *Second* Great Awakening—doesn't make discerning Paul's intentions any easier. In fact, it makes the question all the more difficult.

Almost everyone in the institutional church seems to think highly of Martin Luther, for example. We respect him for challenging the flawed religious systems of his day. But we seem to skip over the underlying catch in giving Luther our admiration: *Didn't Luther's efforts eventually encourage his generation to shift their energies away from the church of their day?*

As Tim Stafford, senior writer at *Christianity Today*, points out, "Until Martin Luther, the church was the immovable center of gravity." More so, "Luther never intended to move that center of gravity. He wanted to purify the church, not defy its authority. Nevertheless, his protests led to schism."[8]

Without sounding too disrespectful, I must confess that the "reformer" in us isn't convinced that pew warming is what gets things done. Would Luther have made the strides he did had he not distanced himself from the church? Was he right to birth a separate movement to try to correct the existing church's flaws? Or should Luther have spent his remaining years patiently praying toward unity with a church who didn't see it his way?

I know, I know. I can hear some of your protests now. "But Luther's situation was entirely different than yours! Luther was combating heresy in a church that was selling salvation for their own financial profit."*

Point taken.

Although, please hear that some twentysomethings feel as if we are defending orthodoxy too. While we may not be overtly concerned with beliefs as they appear on the church books, we are preservationists when it comes to the way churches *live out* Christ's salvation message.

After all, if a congregation even unintentionally targets a very narrow group of people, isn't it excluding other people groups by default? And if the excluded groups perceive the church's salvation message is unavailable to them, that they are not welcome among any given community of believers, then isn't the salvation doctrine being compromised in practice?

To make matters more complex, Luther isn't the only guy who makes leaving the church seem like an attractive option. What about the widely hailed founding fathers of the United States? Should the Puritans and Pilgrims have stuck with the

---

*Luther, a sixteenth-century church Reformer, is most famous for posting his objections —called the Ninety-five Theses—to the door of the castle church in Wittenberg, Germany. Among the major complaints was a protest against the church's practice of selling indulgences—in essence, forgiveness of sin and relief from purgatory. The church of Luther's day believed that purgatory was the place where people, upon their deaths, went to do penance for the sins they had committed and failed to repent of before they died.

Church of England, seeking to act with "one mind" and "one purpose" with their local Christian communities? Would today's current church systems exist if they had?

So some Christians' desire to be part of the church is a conflicted one. One that collides with our disillusionment in some challenging questions: Under what circumstances and to what extent are we to seek unity with existing local churches? And under what circumstances do we strike forward, regarding new movements as reminders of God's fresh involvement with his church?

All of this said, as you can see, many Christians in my generation (and I think it is safe to say, some in other generations as well) can't always claim to be fine. We are not fine with watching our friends and fellow world citizens search for spiritual truth outside of *the* vehicle that Christ himself appointed to dispense it. We are grieved by our peers' absence from the church at large. And we are uncertain about our place in future church history.

It is this state of "not-fineness" that led me to contact you, Church. I wanted to bring the things God is doing in my spirit to expression. To open one more line of communication ... perhaps between my generation and others. Perhaps between the church and multiple generations of its critics. Perhaps between you the people and the very institution you have become.

I write because I myself need the dialogue. I need the opportunity to ask questions. To make observations. To be acknowledged. To learn from others.

And I invite you, the people who are trying to live out the message of the church, into the correspondence because I want to offer you the same opportunity. I want you to know that it is okay if there are times when you aren't fine either. It is okay if your journey is sometimes messy ... if you don't always feel like going to church, if your ideals aren't always grounded in reality, if you can't imagine there being an end to your own disillusionment.

That said, I don't expect you to affirm everything I write is true, Church (because I admit I sometimes write from generational bias, personal experience, or emotion). But I hope some of you might say, "Yes, I understand what you are trying to express" or "I see *why* you feel that way, even if I don't agree with every point you're trying to make."

And finally, I hope that some of you will even respond—perhaps literally at *www.dearchurch.com*—but if not on paper, in your lives.

So, I close this letter with one last request: Write back soon.

Discussion Questions

1. Are the statistics on twentysomething church attendance surprising to you? Why or why not? Explore the reasons why they seem consistent or inconsistent with the attendance patterns in your local church.

2. How does the real-life church match up to your expectations of what church should be?

3. How do you react when church doesn't live up to your ideals?

4. Do you find it easy to accept the church's claim to be "the hope of the world"? Why or why not?

5. If issues surrounding hope are not sources of disillusionment for you, what if anything about the church *does* disappoint you?

6. What are other reasons twentysomethings—or people of any age—might decide to stop attending a church?

7. Why do you think the author says, "I need someone to understand my disillusionment"? Why would she feel she needs someone to relate to her position?

8. Does the author seem conflicted about her generation's departure from the church at large? Are you conflicted when you or others leave the church?

> ## Key Observation
>
> Disillusionment occurs when real life
> doesn't live up to our expectations.

A Fine-Looking Group

Dear Church,

As you've probably noticed, it is hard for me to dialogue about disillusionment without drawing heavily from my own life experiences. While I want to discuss disillusionment broadly, as it applies to *anyone* in *any* life stage, it might be useful to paint a more detailed picture of my generation so you can follow the specifics of my journey with spiritual disappointment.

First of all, let's get formalities out of the way. What should you call us? Ahhhh, we understand your confusion, Church. Sometimes our list of nicknames gets so long, we're near identity crisis ourselves.

Older twentysomethings have been tagged *Generation X*, while younger twentysomethings have been lumped into *Generation Y.** You may also know us as *Baby Busters*, *Echo Boomers*, or *Millennials*.

Not that all our nicknames are positive, mind you. Some call us "kiddults," "twixters," or "adultolescents"—none of which strike me as a compliment. We've also been dubbed the *Slacker Generation*, the *"Me" Generation*, and—in our worst moments—the *"Me! Me! Me!" Generation*.

I, of course, tend to prefer the more favorable reviews, like Neil Howe and William Strauss's description in *Millennials Rising: The Next Generation*, in which they say we are "unlike any

---

*Although experts disagree about who belongs to which generation, Generation X is commonly defined as those born between 1965 and 1980, while Generation Y consists of those born between 1980 and 2001.

other youth generation in living memory."[1] I like the sound of that! But then again, I *could* be a bit biased.

Despite other people's penchant for nicknaming us, though, most twentysomethings are quick to shrug off the titles. Robert Webber, author of *Younger Evangelicals*, was right when he pointed out that young believers don't like being labeled.[2]

My generation's aversion to labels may only make the task of introducing us more difficult. However, I still think it is valuable to familiarize you with some generic features that run in most versions of my generation.

For example, from my experience, twentysomethings are likely to take an interest in human rights. A recent study examining contributions to charities and political causes, *Navigating the Generational Divide in Fundraising and Advocacy*, seems to confirm this. The study found that generations born after 1964 emphasize "'personal' issues such as human rights, family values and civil liberties."[3] Of course, while many of us may feel a need to respond when we see someone's basic human rights being abused, we will not necessarily respond in the same way or with the same intensity.

Take my middle brother, Dave, and me, for example — both of us twentysomething, but with radically different personalities. At times, Dave probably thinks I should undergo some sort of mental evaluation because I seem to dysfunctionally crave edgier life experiences. I've lived and studied in several inner-city areas, including Chicago; I led a canteen unit at Ground Zero; my husband and I purposefully bought a home in a neighborhood where we would be the clear minority race. I stay up all night just thinking and have four-hour-long conversations about things Dave could fit into two sentences.

My reaction to a human rights violation, then, would sound more like some sort of covert op. Parachute into a remote location, free the victims, and overthrow the corrupt regime ... all before lunch, if possible. The more drama, the better!

Dave, on the other hand, excels at being balanced (in a way that is not insulting, but rather grounds people like me from rocketing out of orbit). He teaches at the high school we graduated from, serves in ministry at our dad's church, and married Melissa, who grew up in a neighboring town. Talk about stable!

But despite our differences, Dave would balk at a human rights violation every bit as much as I would. He might teach his high schoolers to be more compassionate world citizens, he might give to organizations that promote relief efforts, and he would definitely pray for those whose rights were being abused. Dave's steady, consistent grace for others speaks volumes about how he believes others should be treated.

If I sat around long enough, I could probably identify a hundred characteristics that could be used to describe my generation. However, in the interest of time and space, I have landed on an even dozen. So, without further delay, let me introduce you to one fine-looking group of somewhat disillusioned young people.

1. Twentysomethings redefine the word *family*.

Perhaps all those feel-good family talks on *Growing Pains* and *Full House* paid off because twentysomethings have emerged as "family people." In 2002, University of Maryland psychologist Jeffrey Jensen Arnett told *Newsweek*, "We are seeing a closer relationship between generations than we have seen since World War II.... Young people genuinely like and respect their parents."[4]

Of course, the twentysomethings' view of family life might be a bit more inclusive than generations past, perhaps because twentysomethings experienced an unprecedented breakdown of the traditional, nuclear family. Many of us were raised in "blended" households where we lived with stepparents, stepbrothers and -sisters, and sometimes half siblings. Survival of the fittest demanded that our generation widen our definition of family to include some who were not genetically related to us.

As a result, we twentysomethings generated our own philosophy of family. We realized that "family" was more about commitment and state of heart than genetic coding. We began expanding our families, building an intimate support group from any number of friends and acquaintances. We invited these perceived "outsiders" into the rawness of our lives, including the low points and breakdowns formerly reserved only for the genetic family behind closed doors.

2. Twentysomethings are comfortable with competing schools of thought.

Thanks to immense technological breakthroughs, twentysomethings have grown up in a "both-and" era. We can get the dinner dishes done *and* still make it to the movie on time, thanks to dishwashers. We can have sex *and* still have reasonable assurance we won't get pregnant, thanks to birth control. And we can overeat *and* lose the pounds, thanks to weight-loss drugs and surgeries. Even more obviously, thanks to email, instant messenger, and cell phones, we can shop, exercise, clean, or drive, *and* still communicate with our friends.

To both our benefit and detriment, our fast-paced culture has seen few limits that innovations cannot stretch. As a result, twentysomethings have not been forced to make as many choices as our predecessors have. Hence, it only follows that we feel like we can have "both-and" in other areas as well.

Politically, for example, many twentysomethings feel like we can be both Republican *and* Democrat, liberal *and* conservative. It's no surprise, then, that according to Gallup, eighteen- to twenty-four-year-olds don't seem to strongly favor any one political pole. On social issues, 36 percent of us claim to be moderate, 36 percent call ourselves liberal, and 27 percent maintain we are conservatives. And even though we lean slightly more liberal than conservative, our conservative values still win out on some issues. According to Gallup, we are no more likely to support some liberal ideas such as abortion rights, feminism, or slacking sexual morals than generations prior.[5]

Younger Americans' real loyalty, then, doesn't seem to lie with a party as much as it lies with an ideal. As noted earlier, twentysomethings lean toward "humanitarian issues," regardless of political affiliation.[6]

This both-and mentality plays out socially, educationally, even spiritually. Twentysomethings feel like we can save the world and still goof off with our friends, use five-syllable words and still enjoy the world's stupidest movies, and live our faith in a way that can be both academically credible *and* emotionally viable, doctrinally sound *and* relationally intelligent.

3. Twentysomethings feel connected to their surroundings.

With the dawn of the computer age, some experts predicted that online chatting and other technology would diminish younger generations' real-life relationships. However, as twentysomethings adapted to our faster and more efficient society, our technology came to have the opposite effect. Not only do we hang out with our friends in person, but thanks to cell phones, email, and instant messenger we also talk to them more frequently in between face-to-face encounters. And even if our friends move to the other side of the country or the other side of the world, we still can stay connected.

Our sense of increased connection isn't just limited to communication with our friends. Because my generation's education included curriculum that focused on environmental, social, and political issues, we have learned to appreciate the invisible umbilical cords that attach us all. Rather than focusing solely on our individuality, twentysomethings have come to value the connection between all the components of our communities (traffic, trees, homes, businesses, etc.). Consequently, if a school is not educating our students, if law enforcement turn their heads at crime, if manufacturers dump waste into our rivers, *we* feel affected because the economy, safety, and health of our community is affected.

We applaud people like Gerald Schlabach, author of *And Who Is My Neighbor?*, who were advocating the value of community before twentysomethings arrived on the planet. As Schlabach says, "Individualism only deepens human poverty."[7]

4. Twentysomethings don't see money as a trustworthy indicator of success.

In a society whose billboards advertise quick divorces for $99 or less, it should come as no surprise that money is the number-one factor cited in the breakup of most marriages. Besides sometimes claiming our parents' marriages, money—or the pursuit of it—occasionally claimed our parents themselves. Overtime became the kidnapper that held our parents hostage. In many cases, having money cost us far more than it afforded.

Raised on an every-other-weekend-shared-holidays schedule, many twentysomethings had two houses, two picket fences, two satellite dishes, *and* two sets of parents. Yet, even our double-your-money American Dream could not guarantee wholesomeness.

Twentysomethings, then, were not surprised by the observations of Potter and Heath, authors of *Nation of Rebels: Why Counterculture Became Consumer Culture*, who found that after a certain point, more money does not necessarily mean more happiness. As twentysomethings know all too well, the extra zeroes in the paycheck don't always pay off. "People are working harder, are under more stress, and are finding themselves with less free time."[8]

That said, I should clarify that twentysomethings aren't anti-money. We like a tall stack of presidents as much as the next generation. But while we still want to find good jobs and be paid what we're worth, we don't want the dollar signs to control us. We are conscious of the dangers that correspond with financial security and we don't want to sacrifice our or our family's emotional health to get it. Perhaps Chris Michalak, human resources consultant for Towers Perrin, says it best: "Baby boomers live to work. Generation Xers work to live."[9]

5. Twentysomethings want instant gratification.

Eric Chester, author of *Employing Generation Why*, made a point to emphasize the twentysomethings' fast pace. "[Members of Generation Y] have been programmed to live life at a rapid pace to keep up with the constant change that is happening around them. They see life as a drop-down menu of choices that can be accessed immediately with the click of a mouse. Speed, change, and uncertainty are normal for Ys."[10]

Chester is right, of course. To notice my generation's obsession with instant gratification, sometimes all you need to do is watch our posture as we wait for our meals in the fast-food line. As we tap our feet, check our watches, and roll our eyes, we say to our friends, "Man, we've been waiting like three minutes. This is the slowest fast-food restaurant on the planet."

Even though life is fast, we're always trying to think of ways to make it faster. My youngest brother, John, who will be twenty on his next birthday, is famous for encouraging the world to speed things along. Ever since he was little, John has evaluated all entertainment venues based on how long it would take us to drive to the necessary location. If I offered to take him to a movie in Toledo — twenty miles south of our Michigan home — John often shrugged off a free ticket and suggested that we settle for whatever flicks were available at the small-town video store just minutes away.

John also repeatedly insists that there should be "citizens' good judgment" laws that would save drivers from having to wait at red lights when no traffic is coming. And just last week, John announced that the restaurant industry should come up with a way to offer fine dining at the same speed some franchises offer fast food.

You probably note by now that being raised in such a quick-delivery environment has equipped twentysomethings with our fair share of humorous deficiencies. Many twentysomethings can be grossly impatient with problems or tasks that cannot be resolved right away. Similarly, we can be famously intolerant of people who don't function as rapidly as we do.

In all the fast-paced mayhem, there are a few positive implications as well. Twentysomethings are inclined to take in information fast, process things immediately, and act on the spot to get things done. Many of us thrive in busy environments.

One way churches can harness twentysomethings' rapid-paced energy is by calling for spontaneous involvement. For instance, rather than scheduling church "work days" for some Saturday two months from now, I've seen a huge response by twentysomethings to last-minute announcements asking, "If anyone can stay after service to help out with this, we would appreciate it." The same thing goes with social get-togethers. When I helped with twenty/thirtysomething small groups at Westwinds Community Church, we often got a good turnout at preplanned social outings. However, the attendance at scheduled events never matched the outpour of people who would join us when we hastily drew maps on the back of our bulletins for impromptu Sunday afternoon picnics or volleyball tournaments.

6. Twentysomethings like technology, but we prefer human contact.

While we're on the subject of instant gratification, let me offer a word of caution to churches that are trying to tune into the twentysomethings' eighty-mile-an-hour techno drive. Thanks to our rapid culture, it can be easy to assume that twentysomethings crave a church of constantly changing flash animation and live-action video footage. But I should let you in on a secret: while twentysomethings appreciate and are familiar with multilayered technology, we are actually very skeptical of our media-driven, advertising-crazed world.

Quite the opposite, twentysomethings want our God and our faith to be different from and *more real than* special effects and airbrushed images on our TV screens. We *don't* want to feel like we worship on an *American Idol* set. We *don't* want the offering spiel to come off like a host introducing the next phase of a reality TV show. And we *don't* want the morning message to rival infomercials with quick promises to improve our lives overnight.

We are seeking the *actual* God—the one who created the entire universe from dust—and we don't think that he has to wait on the next MTV fad or Microsoft update to deliver fresh spiritual experiences.

So please, service design teams, on behalf of twentysomethings everywhere, if you have strobe lights flashing, that's cool. But while the sanctuary is caught up in your makeshift lightning storm, please don't also ask us to watch swirling words or blinking images on a screen. Contrary to some people's beliefs, dizzyness is not the new "cool" way to experience God. Technologically savvy or not, we feel like we just got off a merry-go-round, same as you.

You know what does get our attention? Put real-live humans in front of us and have them tell us about their real lives.

While many twentysomethings roll their eyes at any new label, including *emergent*, emergent church proponents excel at communicating from their real lives. Their emphasis on storytelling goes over well with my generation if it is carried out authentically.

Be careful though. The kind of stories that engage twentysomethings involves more than just Googling the words "funny story" and retelling some amusing online news article as a sermon illustration. As much as we like those clever introductory stories that are designed to grab our attention, we don't usually remember the sermon topic as much as we remember your facial expression as you described what it was like to fly off your four-wheeler into a pile of manure.

On the other hand, tell us what it was like when you had to make a decision about whether or not to marry the person you were dating, tell us about how you persevered after being crushed by some terrible hardship, tell us how you figured out what the heck you were supposed to do with your life, and we will remember what you say forever.

7. Twentysomethings are less relativistic than we seem.

Twentysomethings may confuse our observers. Some days, we may appear to ease through life, entering and exiting multiple worldviews according to our daily whims. Other days, we may need to be physically detached from our soapboxes from which we launch black-and-white declarations about the moral wrongs of our society. I can see confused lay psychiatrists throwing up their hands and diagnosing multiple personalities. "Do the twentysomethings believe in absolutes? Or don't they?"

Does it seem too wishy-washy to say sometimes we do and sometimes we don't?

I'm kidding.

I can certainly see why we may come off as relativistic. But contrary to popular belief, not all twentysomethings keep a copy of *I'm Okay, You're Okay* in our glove compartments.

My generation's ideal world is not one where confusion runs rampant and moral imperatives are near extinction. As one of my fortysomething friends is fond of pointing out, no matter how relativistic any of us may seem, if you break into our garages and steal our cars, we will declare that your worldview—which allows you to take what belongs to me—is completely and totally wrong.

Rather, I'd like to suggest that twentysomethings *do* believe in rights and wrongs. In fact, the strength of some of our opinions might surprise you. *Glamour* magazine, for instance, recently ran an article titled "The Mysterious Disappearance of Young Pro-Choice Women."

According to this article, eighteen- to twenty-nine-year-olds surveyed in a recent CBS/*New York Times* poll were "more conservative about abortion rights than women in every other age category—except women old enough to be their grandmothers, 65 and up!" *Glamour* writer Susan Dominus acknowledged, "This slow but steady seismic shift has gone mostly under the radar, but the reverberations may end up deciding the future of abortion in this country."[11]

8. Twentysomethings are idealistic to a fault.

If you log onto the website for *Delaying the Real World*, a book released in 2005, you will be greeted by the following message:

The Cubicle Can Wait for an Adventure or Two! Congratulations — you've finished school. But if you're not sure you're ready to settle down into an office environment, *Delaying the Real World* is chock-full of creative ideas and practical information that will help you craft your own life-changing adventure:

Teach English in Thailand ◆ Take a road trip ◆ Build houses in a Mexican village ◆ Counsel at a children's art camp ◆ Work on a cruise ship ◆ Lead excursions in the Grand Canyon ◆ Intern at a wildlife sanctuary ◆ Bike (or drive) across America ◆ Guide snorkeling groups in Australia ◆ Hike along the Pacific Trail ◆ Create (and fund) your own service project ◆ Travel around the globe on one affordable plane ticket ◆ And much more![12]

It would be hard to find a better example of my generation's idealism than this book's author: twentysomething Colleen Kinder. Kinder and her book were inspired by twentysomethings who were graduating college, but didn't want to take their place on the starting blocks of the rat race. "I started asking around and I found a lot of people were taking a year to do something that had absolutely nothing to do with their planned career."[13]

As Kinder began further surveying her peers about their postgraduation experiences, she was so fascinated that she began compiling the stories to share with others who were facing the same what-should-I-do-with-my-life decision.

And you don't need to flip through many of these stories to sense a spirit of adventure in the twentysomethings she surveyed. Take Kinder's story about twenty-one-year-old Mary Finnan. Mary dreamed of spending the summer in France, but her meager bank account was not cooperating. Not to be deterred, Mary volunteered to work as a farmhand to a forty-nine-year-old land owner in a remote part of France in order to make the trip a reality.

Portico Research Group, which spent four months studying twenty-one- to twenty-five-year-olds in New York, Chicago, and Los Angeles, found the same thing. They observed that "21–25-year-olds are busy creating a culture of possibility. These young people see every aspect of life as an open opportunity for self-expression and self-fulfillment. Approaching work, fun, friendships, art, music, home decorating and world travel with almost equal levels of enthusiasm and determination, they place their personal stamp upon every endeavor—and expect to learn and grow through each one."[14]

When twentysomethings do buckle down and go to work, Dr. Randall Hansen, webmaster of Quintessential Careers (quintcareers.com), continues to see our trademark flair for idealism. "Twentysomethings around the globe struggle with the transition from college to career—and not just to career, but to the perfect career."[15] (Maybe idealism is why, according to one Senate website, "the average worker leaving college today will switch careers 14 times in their lifetime."[16])

It's no surprise, then, that twentysomethings tend to apply these same idealistic ideas to a search for the perfect church. When we don't find perfection, we can start to get a bit antsy. Hence, people like Craig Dunham, coauthor of *TwentySomeone: Finding Yourself in a Decade of Transition*, have begun studying how the church can retain twentysomethings. And Craig's findings are not especially surprising. In order for these idealistic twentysomethings to plug into churches, Craig says they "need the sense of real responsibility, and the authority needed to accomplish the assigned task."[17]

9. Twentysomethings are transparent.

Eminem is one of the most controversial rap artists of my generation. In fact, he may be one of the most controversial artists of all time. Period.

However, he is also one of the most loved. And he *has been* one of the most loved since his career launched. Eminem was featured in *VIBE, Rolling Stone, Spin,* and *Source* before he even released his first major debut album. By the time that album hit the stores, he was well on his way to developing a diverse fan base powered by every ethnic and socioeconomic group on the census charts. Not to mention Eminem has won seven Grammies and an Oscar.

I know, I know. Eminem's overwhelming popularity blows a lot of people's minds (especially Christians). How could the public adore someone who seems to use the "F-word" to punctuate nearly every sentence he says in public?

I know why. So does Eminem. And so does my generation.

People adore Eminem, or Marshall Mathers III, because he is painfully transparent.

Several years ago, when *Detroit Free Press* music critic Brian McCollum asked Eminem how he got past the intimidation of airing so much dirty laundry on the public airwaves, Eminem responded with his typical candor. "I think one of the reasons is because I make my songs for me. Me and the missus, we go at it. It's no secret we've had our problems, or that we're still having our problems. I feel like when something's bothering me, the best way to get it out is to write a song about it, I think when I do that, people can relate to me more. The more I tell them, the more in touch they are with me."[18]

Eminem may be controversial, and he may say a lot of things that make me cringe, but my generation responds to him with adoration because he doesn't gloss over life's flaws. He is willing to let the world know him for who he is. And twentysomethings and the generation that follows us respect that kind of authenticity.

But you don't have to be a four-letter-word dispenser to be among the transparent role models of our generation. Consider ultraconservative twentysomething Ben Ferguson. Perhaps Eminem's polar opposite, Ben—the youngest nationally syndicated talk show host in history—has acquired his own list of accomplishments. Ben has appeared on the ABC, CNN, and Fox News television networks, and has been featured in the *New York Times*, *Time* magazine, and *Rolling Stone*. Ben also has published a book, *It's My America Too.*[19]

But other than just being well accomplished, the very different Eminem and Ben Ferguson have something else in common. Neither of them pulls any punches.

Ben, for instance, told CNN's Wolf Blitzer that Senator Trent Lott should resign after making a seeming racial comment at Senator Strom Thurmond's one-hundredth birthday and retirement celebration. Some experts thought Ben overreacted, but Ben didn't feel the need to rescind his perhaps politically incorrect but honest remarks. "The best part about doing what I do at such a young age is I don't have to worry about making friends in the business. All the people I could suck up to now won't be around if I need them. I don't have to hold a party line."[20]

This seems to be a fair example of Ben's attitude in general. His profile at Premiere Speakers, the agency that promotes his keynote speaking availability at $7,500 a pop, underlines Ben's transparency. "Ferguson's message is clear. He is not on a campaign to reform liberals and turn them into right-wing Republicans. He is presenting his views on American society and challenging those who do not agree with him to an open debate."[21]

Ben also leaves a similar word for those who are angered by his book: "Don't just get mad. Do something about it."[22]

With both Eminem and Ben, what you see is what you get. And that's what twentysomethings like—in their role models and in their churches.

Perhaps Mike Sares, pastor at Scum of the Earth Church in Denver, Colorado, says it best: "Twentysomethings don't want 'the victorious Christian life,' they want to be allowed to struggle. When the pastor, the Sunday school teacher, or the Bible study leader speak (week after week) about how things *ought* to be without telling the church how badly they themselves have blown it, young adults write them off as inauthentic." On the contrary, Mike notes that one of the highest compliments a pastor can receive is to have a congregation member learn from his struggles and go on believing that "they, too, can fail and still keep following Jesus."[23]

(No, Scum of the Earth Church is not a typo. Go check it out for yourself at *www.scumoftheearth.net*.)

10. Twentysomethings value community.

I most notice my generation's drive for community when we attempt to form small groups. Over the past seven years, I have been part of several twentysomething small groups. So many, in fact, that I have a hard time remembering exactly how many groups I've been a part of or who even attended which group.

Maybe the groups blur together because the twentysomethings in our church never fully embraced the textbook small-group model. In fact, we broke every rule in our dust-collecting Small Group Leader's Manual. We did not stay on topic. We let people drone on about their personal issues for hours. We cried. We prayed. We held heated debates (among our favorites was an intense argument over the likelihood of flying cars). We hardly ever completed our entire discussion of the week's curriculum. And although we managed a couple of dinner outings over the course of many years, we certainly didn't fill our calendar with scheduled small-group events.

Worst of all, we never quite got the group-birthing process down smoothly. Sure, we birthed new small groups in an effort to multiply, but somehow, the same people seemed to cycle in and out of all of them. No one had perfect attendance, but everyone seemed to show up at least irregularly. At least one girl I know of even went to more than one small group so she could keep in touch with everyone.

Eventually, whether it was small-group season or not and whether we were listed in the directory or not, the twentysomethings were hanging out so regularly that the small groups themselves kind of melted into the background.

Every Sunday we crossed paths constantly while serving as church greeters or in children's ministry. As we passed each other, we would exchange knowing smiles and feelings of enthusiasm for the causes we were teamed in. Sometime during the morning, at least one twentysomething—often a different person each week—would take the initiative to ask, "So, are we doing anything after church today?"

The answer was almost always yes. Although we rarely did any preplanning during the week, the twentysomethings routinely set aside Sunday afternoons to hang out together.

Before you knew it, we were borrowing black Sharpies from the information table and sketching off-scale maps to our chosen meeting location on the backs of bulletins or offering envelopes or whatever else was available. After photocopying our makeshift maps into even poorer quality duplicates, we would hand them out to anyone we knew who was even remotely tied to our age group. (Our twentysomething group was often referred to as the twenty/thirtysomething group, but no one noticed when people on either end of the continuum stretched the age limit even past that.)

On the bottom of our maps we would inevitably scribble any other necessary information for participating in the day's events. One common addition was the reminder to bring snacks of some kind. Whatever we were doing, whether it was playing football or volleyball, watching *Star Wars* marathons, or playing board games, it always required food.

We never bothered to organize an official hospitality team. Instead, our meals were more like the smorgasbords a family has the night before Mom goes grocery shopping—everybody just kind of eats what they can find. And so one person might bring two chicken breasts and another a steak—yes, one steak—and yet another a pack of hotdogs. Our favorite components—potato chips with sour cream dip, tortilla chips and salsa, and Ruby Red Squirt—were so simple they wouldn't even qualify as a potluck.

But don't think twentysomethings' drive for community is centered around impromptu sporting events and food. There were plenty of real-life decisions and hassles to walk through together as well. Whether the issue was dating, illness, death, or depression, there was a seemingly endless list of situations that forced us to dig deep and learn hard spiritual truths that strengthened our relationships even further.

So we enjoy small-group community. But who doesn't? Ahhh, but our expressions of community go much further than that. The building where my two best friends and I led a women's small group eventually became home to ten of us—April, Jennie, Bethany, Diane, Scott, Melanie, Amanda, Nate, Melissa, and myself—who at one time or another lived in the two upstairs apartments. In addition, over the course of a few years, seven different people with connections to our twentysomething group worked at the mental-health organization where I worked in college. Finally, if I'm counting correctly, this same group has attended, participated in, or helped set up/tear down at least ten church-related twentysomething weddings. In my wedding alone, former small-group members served as bridesmaids, band members, decorators, and even one of the pastors!

While we may have failed our small-group test, our coaches hardly ever felt the need to check in with us.

And with good reason.

Twentysomethings are lovers of community.

11. Twentysomethings want to help.

About a month ago, my friend Sarah Burkel was standing in line waiting to purchase an item at a Detroit-area electronics store.

Like most people, Sarah had plenty of other things she wanted to do that day and was hoping that she would be able to quickly check out and get on with her to-do list.

No such luck.

For whatever reason, one customer's transaction was taking forever.

Several minutes later, when the cashier finally closed the drawer and handed the receipt to the woman who had been ahead of Sarah, the female customer became increasingly distressed.

As Sarah waited even longer, she could overhear the dialogue as the lady—whose thick accent gave away her Eastern origin—explained that she had missed the city bus and would now have to walk home with the stereo she had just purchased.

As Sarah imagined this lady, apparently unaccustomed to life in the US, lugging a stereo back to her home several miles away, she contemplated whether it was wise to offer the stranger a ride. Unfortunately, the woman exited the store before Sarah had a chance to come to a decision. A bit disappointed, but also relieved from having to extend herself, Sarah hopped into her car and began driving home—a drive that would have been a short trip had she not immediately passed the woman, trying to balance the stereo on her hip as she meandered home on foot.

Sarah pulled over to give the woman a ride, but from there her endeavor got more complicated. It turned out the woman didn't know how to get back to her home by car. She only knew the bus route. Sarah was undeterred. In following what little information they had, the two of them worked together to find their way back to the woman's apartment.

Along the way, Sarah and the woman talked about all kinds of things, from family to faith. It turned out, this woman was living in a practically empty apartment by herself as she worked to try to earn enough money to bring her husband and children to the United States to join her.

That day, she confessed, she had been so lonely she had finally broken down and gone to the store to purchase a CD player so her sparse apartment wouldn't always sound so quiet and lonely.

Of course, what could have been a disastrous walk home immersed in even deeper loneliness became an uplifting connection, thanks to Sarah's willingness to go out of her way for a stranger who had been holding up the line in front of her.

Twentysomethings like Sarah want to help.

From Danny Seo, the twentysomething environmentalist who started a teenage-driven charity to preserve the world's environment, to the bloggers and coffee shop customers who lent a hand in the formation of these letters, twentysomethings want to contribute to the larger community.

This particular attribute, this desire to help, has been frequently noticed by experts who have studied younger generations in depth.

Eric Chester, author of *Employing Generation Why*, also noticed that volunteerism was at an all-time high, "thanks to the unprecedented involvement of Generation Y, who are putting their time where their hearts are. It is hard to find an organized student club, sport, or activity where participants aren't involved in some type of community service as a part of their credo. Soccer teams stick around after their games to help clean up the park. Student councils visit nursing homes, paint homes for the elderly, and hold canned food drives. Cheerleaders volunteer to take underprivileged children trick or treating."[24]

Robert Putnam, author of *Bowling Alone*, also concludes: "A wide range of evidence also suggests that young Americans in the 1990s displayed a commitment to volunteerism without parallel among immediate predecessors."[25]

12. Twentysomethings don't pledge our allegiance lightly.

While on staff at Westwinds Community Church, we noticed this slow-to-commit trend almost by accident. Despite being active in our church for a couple years, one of our well-known twentysomething volunteers seemed to be purposely avoiding the church's membership process. At first, as the staff tried to determine how to proceed, some suggested that perhaps he was just trying to be anti-institutional. But the more we talked to him, the more we understood a principle that would later manifest itself in the leadership lives of several twentysomethings.

This guy was not antiestablishment. He just didn't want to formally commit to membership until he was absolutely convinced that he wanted to be fully committed to the church.

And church isn't the only thing we're slow to commit to.

Twentysomethings wait longer to commit to marriage than previous generations. New data from the 2004 US census population survey tells us that today's average woman gets married at age twenty-six while the average man gets married at twenty-seven, as opposed to 1970 when women got married around age twenty and men got married at about twenty-three.

As follows, twentysomethings hold off on committing to parenthood as well. In 2000, the average woman was almost twenty-five years old when her first child was born, as opposed to 1970 when the average woman gave birth for the first time around 21.4 years of age.[26]

To the frustration of companies around the world, twentysomethings are equally slow to commit to brand-name products. Hence the reason Toyota had to rebrand an entire new line, the Scion, and require their dealers to pay $25,000 in training fees to learn how to effectively sell cars to our generation.[27]

The church need not be offended by twentysomethings' hesitation to commit. Everybody, from Pepsi to the Republicans to the United States Army, is trying to figure out how to get younger generations to shift their allegiance.

If you have the patience to wait for us, though, you'll find that we become loyal investors in the end. As Ann Fishman, president of Generational Targeted Marketing Corporation, claims, members of Generation Y do eventually become brand loyal. However, their loyalty only comes *after* they have been allowed to discover the brands through their own devices, such as peer recommendations or self-guided investigations over the Internet.[28]

« »

Now that I've described these twelve traits, I'll close this letter the same way I started—by noting that twentysomethings don't like being categorized.

I am no exception, a fact that comes out in areas as simple as my dress code.

I know that one day I may appear to be a tomboy who likes to toss around a football, while the next I come off a crisp middle-class professional. And still, a third day, I may strike you as so comfortable in my grocery store gear—pajama pants and flannel shirts—that I seem to think the world is my backyard. But to me, these variations are not contradictory. I *am* all of these things. And I *want* to be all of these things. I would never want to be just one of them.

Similarly, twentysomethings would rather not be considered postmodern or emergent, or Y or X, or any other label with any permanence just because of our age.

And perhaps the greatest reason twentysomethings don't want to be labeled is that we don't want to be known for who we are now. We want to be known for who we are striving to be. For who we are becoming.

That said, I want to warn you. Even though I've described my generation, don't think I've done all the work for you.

Granted, to increase my own credibility, I have attempted to choose characteristics that represent a broader group than just my own friends by sharing my ideas with large numbers of twenty-something contacts in real life and online. However, despite my best efforts, I know that I can't possibly account for all the variation within my generation.

This is exactly why the business world encourages companies to think about their specific customers rather than reading into generalizations. This seems to be good advice for the church as well. If you're a leader in your local church, then please—by all means—get to know the twentysomethings in *your* community. Toss them a copy of this letter, if you like, and ask them to tell you whether they relate to the characteristics described here. And if they want to critique my characterization of twentysomethings, then hear them out. This will only further serve to clarify things I might have missed.

Lastly, I bet if you *do* take the time to sit down with a real-live twentysomething, you will discover at least one additional trait of my generation.

Just to forewarn you: we tend to be opinionated.

Discussion Questions

1. What labels have you most heard applied to twentysomethings? What labels have been applied to other generations?
2. Why do people feel the need to label specific age groups? What is the purpose of labels?
3. Do you think labels are helpful in understanding new generations? Explain.
4. Why do you think that twentysomethings' position on controversial issues such as abortion might develop under the radar?
5a. Which of the characteristics that the author describes have you seen in twentysomethings? Explain how certain traits are noticeable to you.
5b. If you are not a twentysomething, to which of the characteristics of the twentysomethings do you most relate? To which do you least relate?
6. Which twentysomething characteristics do you see as most beneficial? Which seem most harmful?
7. Which characteristics might make twentysomethings more susceptible to disillusionment with the institutional church?
8. How do you see some of these characteristics contributing to the future church as it evolves?

Key Observation

Allowing others to get to know you and understand the
influences that shaped you may help them empathize
and respond to your concerns.

part 2

Introducing
Disillusionment

No Gatekeepers

Dear Church,

I know you've probably heard your share of cheesy religious jokes that are cleverly woven into sermons or repeated in your hallways. But I have one more for you.

A woman died and was instantly transported to the pearly gates just outside heaven's entrance. St. Peter promptly greeted her and almost immediately launched into his well-rehearsed orientation, ending with the statement, "So all you have to do is perform one task correctly and you will be granted entrance into eternity with God."

"A task?" the woman repeated nervously. "Well, okay. I don't know how I'll do, but I'll obviously give it my best."

"Ahhhh, it's not so bad." St. Peter smiled. "All you have to do is spell *love*."

The woman sighed in relief and quickly answered, "L-o-v-e."

"Congratulations! You're in." St. Peter applauded. Then looking curiously at her, he asked, "Hey, you wouldn't believe how long I've been standing here. Would you mind just watching the counter for a few minutes while I slip out and run a couple of errands?"

Not wanting to seem ungenerous on her first day in heaven, the woman immediately agreed.

As she awaited St. Peter's return, the woman's ex-husband approached the pearly gates. Seeing who was at the counter made him noticeably anxious.

"Don't worry," she said soothingly, "all you have to do is perform one task correctly and you will be granted entrance into heaven."

"Anything," he said. "What do I have to do?"

"Spell *chrysanthemum*."

We repeat cheesy little religious jokes like this to get a good laugh, but of course we never claim that doctrinal truth is involved. We don't really expect to see a *human* gatekeeper standing between us and heaven when we die. A fair and merciful God could never allow imperfect, biased humans to take on such a weighty task.

Why is it, though, I sometimes wonder, are we Christians so capable of recognizing this flaw—that there is no human gatekeeper to God's kingdom—as it applies to the afterlife, but seemingly less capable of realizing the same truth this side of heaven?

There are no human gatekeepers in the kingdom. God has never and will never hire a flawed person to judge whether someone else qualifies to approach him or claim allegiance to him. Acts 10:42 tells us that Jesus is the judge of the living and the dead.

And yet many of us probably know a few members of a rebel elitist Christian force who, perhaps trying to be helpful, have taken it upon themselves to pass out tickets to those they feel belong in God's kingdom. *One for you, one for you, and ... um, you ... oops, we seem to have run out of tickets. Please check back never.*

And, just like in the joke, when flawed humans dictate who belongs, inevitably some people or people groups—who don't meet certain predetermined criteria—get a lesser welcome into Christian community. As a result, they are pushed to the outskirts of mainstream Christianity or may never choose to explore our local congregations at all. This is a source of disillusionment for many.

"When I look out and see a congregation where everyone is the same race and socioeconomic status, something in my heart drops," author Margaret Feinberg recently told me in an email. "Something longs deep inside of me. There has to be more. I think this is one of the aches of our generation: to see the diversity with which God creates the body of Christ translated into our churches."

Margaret should know. I sought her insight largely because of two qualifications. First of all, in the process of writing *Twentysomething, How to Be a Grown-Up*, and other titles, Margaret interviewed dozens and dozens of twentysomethings. Second, though—and perhaps more important—Margaret doesn't just write about twentysomethings, she is one.

When it comes to a more inclusive church, Margaret and I are on the same page. We both believe that integrating more diverse people groups into our church communities should be a central goal for our generation. And really, it is not an issue that emerged only as we entered adulthood. Our expectations concerning relationships with diverse people groups have been a long time forming.

Think about the status of the world when our generation arrived post–Civil Rights movement. Though race and economic relations were still far from perfect, the US was starting to look and feel very different. Our history books, for instance, featured Martin Luther *and* Martin Luther King Jr., George Washington *and* George Washington Carver, Andrew Jackson *and* Jesse Jackson.

Multiple ethnic and economic groups learned in the same classrooms during the school year and swam in the same pools during the summer. We drank at the same drinking fountains and ordered kids' meals at the same restaurants. On our buses, *everyone* wanted to ride in the back because that was the seat farthest away from the driver.

In elementary school, we were glued to the TV set every Thursday night to watch *Bill Cosby*. Every morning, Al Roker told us about the weather in "our neck of the woods" and every evening, Connie Chung wished us a good night. And though we may or may not have been allowed to listen to them, we were avid followers of bra-baring Janet, and Michael, the one-gloved moonwalker.

We got our education on multiculturalism from *Different Strokes*, *Facts of Life*, and *Webster* before we ever enrolled in high school sociology. And we learned our first foreign languages from Maria and the other friendly neighbors on *Sesame Street*.

As we grew older, we had crushes on *Saved by the Bell* characters Lisa Turtle and A. C. Slater and memorized the theme song to Will Smith's *Fresh Prince of Bel-Air*. We thought that M. C. Hammer was too legit to quit, that Ahmad Rashad had the inside stuff, and that Arsenio Hall would one day replace Letterman. We borrowed our first karate moves from Bruce Lee and Jackie Chan and toured our first colleges with Denise Huxtable and Dwayne Wayne. And Gatorade's commercial was right on: we wanted to be like Mike because Mike made us believe we could fly.

By default, twentysomethings are the most integrated generation raised in the Western world to date. Yet our appetite for integrating diverse people into our relational circles isn't limited to the Western Hemisphere.

As our local culture grew more diverse, the twentysomethings' world also grew more similar. We were somehow naturalized into the global village without ever applying for citizenship.

Our routines came to include regular virtual walks in other people's shoes, courtesy of now-considered-educational TV. We looked on as tanks ravaged Tiananmen Square, the Berlin Wall crumbled, and Patriot missiles collided with Iraqi targets. We frowned, we cheered, and we frowned again ... unaware that we were being slowly integrated into a global culture from the comfort of our classrooms.

And the older we got, the more the world came to us. Before we knew it, we could meet, chat, email, date, and witness to people from an expanding list of countries via the World Wide Web. If we did want to see the world firsthand, that became more doable too. Travelocity, Orbitz, Expedia, and CheapTickets.com brought intense competition to the airline industry and offered travelers discounted fares that were previously purchased only by the well-off.

For good and bad, diversity and global thinking snuck into our political scene too. Magic Johnson lobbied for AIDS research. Rosie supported gay adoptions. Bono advocated for third world relief. And Superman (aka Christopher Reeve) pushed the issue of stem cell research. Affirmative action, handicap accessibility, religious postings in public buildings, and civil unions became matters for the courts to decide.

As you can see, for those of us raised in such a diverse and integrated society, adopting a more inclusive approach to everyday life was not just an option but — at some level — a necessity for survival.

Now, as we wander into the arena of adults, our world is no less diverse. While roughly three-fourths of United States' citizens still identify themselves as "white," Hispanic and Asian populations are growing at much faster rates than other groups.[1] Not only have African, Mexican, Chinese, Filipino, Asian, Indian, Brazilian, Pakistani, Albanian, Honduran, *and* Trinidadian and Tobagonian populations grown since 1990, some of them doubled.[2] In addition, a full 11.7 percent of the current US population were born in a foreign country.[3]

Diversity is not just a racial issue. Family arrangements are becoming more varied. Twenty-seven percent of children are raised in single-parent households; 5 percent live in homes with neither parent present.[4] Physically speaking, 49.7 million people in the US live with some type of long-lasting condition or disability, meaning that nearly one in five* citizens are categorized as disabled.[5] And linguistically, 17.9 percent speak at least one language other than English, while 10 percent don't speak English at all.[6]

Educationally, the US continues to be dominated by three different groups: as of 2000, 27 percent of adults had earned their

*This figure is likely even larger because it does not include those living in prisons, nursing homes, and other institutions.

bachelor's degree, 85 percent had earned a high school diploma or equivalency, and 15 percent had not completed high school.[7] Economically, Americans also find themselves in three primary groups: almost half of households make between $25,000 and $75,000 per year, 28 percent make under $25,000, and 22.5 percent make more than $75,000.[8]

This diversity streak is not about to fade either, Church. Nonwhites already outnumber whites in California, but by 2050, the whole country is projected to be dominantly nonwhite.[9]

To twentysomethings nursed and immersed in such a mixed culture, nothing makes more sense than grooming churches that are intentionally inclusive of society's diverse people groups.

In this department, however, we are sometimes grossly disappointed. Churches are not always perceived as welcoming ... especially to groups of people unlike the majority of their attenders.

I am not surprised by the observations of author and speaker Marilyn Brenden, who writes: "Usually the cause [behind why people leave church groups] originates from one of two things: a failure of the group to assimilate the person or personal issues in the class member's life. Unfortunately, when a class has been together for a long time, the 'old' members may cluster together in an exclusive huddle. New members feel a barrier in trying to join in. As one new member put it, 'They drew a circle and left me out.'"[10]

At some level, I think I've always been at least somewhat aware of this type of exclusion in the church. I remember very clearly, for example, the day a longtime friend pulled me aside after church one Sunday. We were twelve years old.

"Sarah, my parents said I can't hang out with you as much anymore," she whispered, as she eyed the hallway for any adult spies.

"What?!"

"They think you're going down the wrong path."

I guess my look of disbelief conveyed what I was thinking, because my friend quickly continued at about eighty miles an hour. "I tried to tell them that you were the most Christian kid I knew and you knew a lot about the Bible and were always witnessing to people, but they wouldn't listen. I guess one of the other parents told them you were hanging out too much with Keith and Jessica.* A lot of the parents don't think they are good influences."

"That is crazy," I responded. It was true that Keith and Jessica weren't raised in the church and that their backgrounds were much different than mine, but despite their flaws, they were—at least in my mind—experiencing spiritual growth that would stack up against that of any deacon or usher. "Do they realize that Keith and Jessica come to church completely on their own? No one wakes them up on Sundays and makes them come."

"Yeah, that's part of the problem. The parents think they talk too much in church services and that they run around the building unsupervised. They think they might have been the ones who cracked the outlet covers in the fellowship hall." (No, you didn't read wrong; back then we closely tracked anyone who so much as laid a finger on our plastic electrical socket covers.)

"Anyway, that's not the worst of it. One of the other fathers told my dad that there is a rumor going around that you and Keith were having sex."

I stared back at her, by now registering complete shock. As I slowly internalized the church's disapproval, I managed a few words of protest. "I haven't even held a guy's hand ..."

"I know, I told them you were like the Virgin of the Century, but they didn't care. They told me I need to back off hanging out with you for a while." Then, before she walked away, she added, "I think it's really because Angela's parents are afraid that she will go out with Keith. They told her that Keith doesn't come from a good background and they don't want her getting mixed up with him."

At twelve years old, I learned an important underground lesson that ran contrary to some of those that ran from the pulpit. It

*Not their real names.

seems there are sometimes unwritten, whispered rules about who does and doesn't belong in church.

By the time I hit adulthood, I had seen enough similar incidents that I began to feel particularly embarrassed by the church's short-armed evangelical reach. A moment of particularly memorable shame occurred during one of two semesters that I lived in a southside Chicago homeless shelter. It was here that I ran into Nancy.*

An ultra-intelligent nurse with two master's degrees, Nancy had only recently skied down a slippery slope into homelessness. It all started when Nancy's husband left her and she married the bottle. Her faithfulness to alcohol caused her to lose control of her own emotions and health. Eventually, she was deemed an unfit mother, which resulted in even more drinking. It wasn't long before Nancy wasn't going to work, wasn't paying her bills ... then, seemingly overnight, she was homeless.

As I listened to Nancy articulately retell the events of the last year, I was confident that at one time she would have blended into the row of *Good Housekeeping* wives in my hometown church. She would have had a favorite song to request from the worship band, a trademark dish to bring to potlucks, and a steady Thursday evening small group that scrapbooked together. With her charismatic personality and animated hand gestures, she would have made the perfect third-grade vacation Bible school teacher.

Now, thanks to her unstyled hair, chipped fingernails, and chain smoking, Nancy would be virtually invisible to many churchgoers. If she did, by chance, run into people who might have passed the offering basket to her on previous Sundays, it would probably be to ask them for change for the subway. And somehow I knew, even if they gave her the entire contents of their wallets, not many of them would give her relationship. Not many would stop to engage her the way they might have in her previous state.

*Not her real name.

What did this say about the church? I asked myself. And just as important, *what did this say about me?* I didn't want to believe that something as simple as Nancy's shift in social status had single-handedly decreased the likelihood of her being accepted by a church. And I didn't want to believe that something as simple as disheveled clothing and unkempt hair would prevent me from building a meaningful relationship with a person.

I still don't want to believe that.

Sighhhhhhhh.

If I was honest with myself, though, I knew that my routine, real-life witness didn't comfortably extend to people like Nancy. My real "witness," the kind of witness that evolves when you invest years in relationship with the same people, was mostly restricted to my group of friends. People I already knew. People who were *like me.*

I hate to break it to you, Church, but I'm not the only one who isn't well equipped to build relationships with diverse people groups. Take a look at the racial makeup of our local congregations, for instance. Research led by Dr. Michael Emerson, co-author of *Divided by Faith* and *Sociology of Religion*, shows that only about 7 percent of all American congregations are multiracial. Focus solely on Protestant movements and the numbers dip even lower. Only 5 percent of Protestant congregations are multiracial.[11]

But let's not get hung up on just the race card.

As Tom Huang, an editor at the *Dallas Morning News*, points out, young people's subcultures—such as hip hop, skateboarding, Anime, video games, and extreme sports—are "beginning to transcend race."[12]

Likewise, there are other groups—outside of racial ones—that should be on the church's radar too. While completing my urban studies minor, I made lists of other people groups who were seemingly missing in action from the white middle-class churches I attended growing up. These people included, but were not limited to addicts, adult entertainment employees, AIDS victims, blue-collar workers, divorcees, those suffering from eating disorders, the elderly, foster care children, gangs, goths, the homebound, the homeless, homosexuals, the hospitalized, the illiterate, immigrants, low-income families, the mentally ill, minority races, the non-English speaking, the physically challenged, pregnant teens, prisoners, those dependent on public transportation, runaways, the socially challenged, single parents, skaters, unwed mothers, the undereducated, the unemployed, vegans, the visually impaired, those dependent on welfare, and widows/widowers.

But let me slow up a bit.

Before I congratulate myself for observing so many diverse people groups, let me offer a quick disclaimer, Church. I can't take the credit. The whole inclusion thing? Wasn't my idea. I borrowed it. Straight-out plagiarized it from another world leader.

The diverse people groups Jesus interacted with included, but were not limited to men, women, children, shepherds, wise men from foreign countries, fishermen, synagogue officials, the diseased, the demon-possessed, those prone to seizures, the paralyzed, lepers, centurions, the blind, the mute, zealots, Pharisees, Sadducees, hometown citizens, teachers of the law, physicians, tax collectors, the rich, the chief priests, soldiers, governors, thieves, widows, prostitutes, beggars, kings, wedding guests, public officials, Jews, Canaanites, Samaritans, and Syrophoenicians.

While I don't know if Jesus' social routine was meant to be descriptive (just a record of what happened in his life) or prescriptive (an example that we should follow), I am pretty comfortable erring on the side of Jesus on this one. I mean if you're going to copy someone, he's a good bet, don't you think, Church?

Besides the prospect of missing out on a facet of Jesus' mission, the exclusive church could come off uncomfortably similar to a snobby fraternity.

Not that I'm comparing church behavior to the actions of those who are perhaps best known for sucking up too much hard liquor. Rather, I'm thinking about the processes that must be undertaken when a person tries to belong—to move from the fringes of the organization to the inner circle.

Local congregations, of course, have varied requirements for membership; however, many of them still seem to stand in contrast to Jesus' approach. The only task that Jesus mentioned, when asked what God required of people, is "to *believe* in the one he has sent."

It was *belief* that made someone a disciple (John 8:31), *belief* that deemed them God's children (John 1:12), and *belief* that qualified them as children of Abraham (Galatians 3:7). *Belief* was also the qualifier that got tax collectors and prostitutes to the door before religious leaders (Matthew 21:31–32).

Throughout the New Testament, we see this same mode of entry revisited by author after author. Paul reminded people that the Spirit doesn't move because you observe the law, but because you *believe* what you've heard (Galatians 3:5). Peter taught it was only through *belief* in God that people had hope (1 Peter 1:21). John too passed on a similarly simple command: *believe* in the name of God's Son, Jesus Christ, and love one another as he commanded us (1 John 3:23). Even the chief priests and Pharisees feared that if Jesus continued to do miracles, more people would *believe* (John 11:48). In fact, belief was apparently such a central part of Christians' identities that they were referred to as *believers* (Acts 4:32 is just one example).

Interestingly enough, from Nicodemus (John 3) to Zacchaeus (Luke 19), the Samaritan townspeople (John 4:39–42) to the disciples (Matthew 4, Mark 3, Luke 5, John 1), not one person is asked to sign a list of doctrines.

In fact, there is no "repeat after me." No "raise a hand." No "ask Jesus into your heart."

Just believe.

And you know what is cool about belief? It's something anyone can do. Physically disabled, mentally challenged, young, old, smart, uneducated. Not everyone can understand and recite a list of complex doctrines, not everyone can read and process a manual. But even a child can *believe*.

I once worked with a homeless man who was both schizo-phrenic and epileptic. Because of his mental illness, he came to think that men he was once imprisoned with had implanted a homing device in the back of his head and were tracking his every move (it sounds bizarre, but real life is sometimes). When-ever something would go wrong—for example, if a salt shaker would get bumped off the table—this man would chalk it up as evidence that the cons were following him and out to make his life miserable. You can only imagine the chaos and confusion that ruled him.

My husband and I went to all lengths to help this man and his wife. We secured temporary housing for them in a hotel and made a return trip to argue with the staff when they tried to evict him. We searched out an apartment in the city where he and his wife could walk to nearby organizations that could support them. We took him, his wife, and his dog (that he refused to leave be-hind) to our church on a number of occasions.

Despite all of our efforts, I never heard this man engage con-version by the definitions of my childhood. Even if the perfect moment had presented itself, he would have never—in my wild-est dreams—been able to process the beliefs inherent in most of the creeds and church covenants I'd been raised on. But the lon-ger we talked, the more often my husband and I heard the man say, "I think they are following me, but I know they won't get to me because God is watching out for me" or "When they come near, I just ask God to help me."

Less than a year after coming into our lives, this man died suddenly (his wife claimed paramedics didn't even attempt to resuscitate him after he had a seizure). As I sat at the funeral, looking at the man's body in the coffin, a new spiritual principle dawned on me. I thought to myself: without a doubt, this man is experiencing Christ's fullness right now. Like Abraham, like the centurion, like those who ate and fellowshiped with the early church, this man *believed*.

Of course "just believe" is a little too simple for some theologians. Some critics will surely say, "But aren't church doctrines important? Shouldn't we try to know them?" Unquestionably yes. I know them and I advocate knowing them. After all, we are transformed by the renewing of our minds (Romans 12:2).

"And how will we know if someone believes?"

They will bear fruit.

"But how will we judge if they have enough fruit?"

We're not supposed to judge. (Coincidentally, Jesus put the nix on judging in the same Matthew 7 message, right before he mentioned the fruit part.)

The moment a person believes, he or she becomes part of the church. Whether or not they ever attend or belong to a local church, whether or not they ever read or sign off on a membership manual, their names are instantly uploaded into the global church's membership list. If they join one local congregation but later leave to join another, there should be no need to send a letter of transfer.

Even without the gift of discernment, you can probably guess by my "fraternity" comparison or my "just believe" salvation message that not everyone applauds me when I open my mouth about the church. And you'd be right. Especially in my younger days, as I expressed my desire to see the church become more inclusive, it often seemed like I needed an interpreter to translate my thoughts to other age groups in the church at large.

First of all, I (along with many of my peers) often become so passionate about my position and so raw with my critiques, that my words become isolating, if not exhausting. I became the ambassador of the twentysomething people of Planet Cynicism.

Second, I found that words like *diversity* or *multiculturalism*, which are dominantly positive words in the eyes of my peers, incite panic in others. To some, the word *multicultural* is linked to a sinfully liberal political agenda and to others, the word *diversity* screams relativism.

Third, some just wrote me off as emotionally driven, relationally needy, and in search of warm fuzzies that come with swaying to "Lean on Me" while holding hands with people in the ghetto.

Let me give you an example of one of the statements I made early on that raised many an okay-that-might-be-true-but-you-still-shouldn't-have-said-it eyebrow. I have often noted, for example, that I could go to an Eminem concert and put my hands in the air ("everybody in the 313, put your hands up and follow me") alongside every socioeconomic and racial group in the US. Yet if I go to church the next day, I point out, I'd be raising my hands with a thousand other people of the same race and general social class.

Do I say this because I like to incite controversy? Um, well, maybe just a little.

But, do I say this because I'm political? Because I'm a relativist? Because I have a penchant for swaying to cheesy songs? No. The real question is not, "How can we get the church to be more like an Eminem concert?" (which, by the way, doesn't have a wide age sampling despite its economic and racial diversity). The more important question is, "What does the lack of diversity in many churches show us about the condition of our hearts and the effectiveness of our collective mission?"

The church's ability to engage its diverse world is not a political issue, it's a missional issue. An obedience issue. A do-you-take-Jesus'-parting-shot-to-his-disciples-seriously issue.

The heart of the matter is not *racial* or *economic* reconciliation, but *spiritual* reconciliation.

Just as "giving our lives to Christ" involves shifting our allegiance each day we wake up, one day at a time, "going into all the world" involves being the church to each person we encounter, one person at a time. Eventually, if we make it through enough people, we are — by default — destined to run into some people unlike ourselves. The road to reaching the world, then, runs straight through the middle of diverse people groups.

One last thing, Church: Maybe if we gave up controlling who and how people belong, we would teach people that *we* are not the givers of salvation or the gatekeepers of the kingdom. And maybe, if they came to see salvation being extended and maintained by God, they would be a whole lot less disillusioned with us.

Just a thought.

I've got to think about this some more.

Discussion Questions

1. Does lack of diversity in a church congregation bother you? Why or why not? (Keep in mind that diversity is much broader than just race or skin color.)
2. As a child, were you exposed to different people groups via television or other forms of media? If so, how, if at all, do you think it affected you? If not, how, if at all, do you think the lack of exposure affected your worldview?
3. Do you believe the church "system" will have to change in order to build relationships with increasingly diverse people groups? Why or why not?
4. In your experiences, what are the whispered, underground rules about who does or doesn't belong in church?
5. Has interacting with someone like Nancy ever caused you to reevaluate your witnessing strategy? If so, please explain.
6. Why do you think churches tend to add to Jesus' bottom-line requirement of belief?

Key Observation

When we Christians become too controlling of our institutions, those hurt by our flawed initiatives are likely to direct their disillusionment with individuals toward the entire church ... or, worse yet, toward God.

Stonewashed Churches

Dear Church,

Those of you who have been in church circulation since the mid-nineties may remember a couple of reports that put America's church-attendance figures under the global microscope.

Although several pollsters reported that roughly 40 percent of Americans attended church, not everyone agreed with their findings. Articles like the *American Sociological Review*'s "What the Polls Don't Show: A Closer Look at U.S. Church Attendance," claimed the number of church attenders was much smaller—maybe as low as 20 percent. The 40 percent statistic, the new studies claimed, was exaggerated because the people surveyed often felt pressured to lie concerning socially desirable behavior like church attendance.[1]

I wasn't aware of the disputes about church attendance numbers until a long time after this particular report's release date (at the time it was released I think I was in tenth grade and a bit more interested in the guy on my track team than in the *Sociological Review*). When I did get wind of the report though, I had to wonder why the church attendance statistics for my generation were so low—despite this apparent pressure to be perceived as socially desirable. Were we just not smart enough to lie on the surveys like everyone else? (Darn it, twentysomethings, next time exaggerate a bit more!)

I say that tongue-in-cheek, not to suggest that my generation has higher standards when it comes to truth-telling, but to suggest some of us have big mouths and a tendency to tell it like it is. Or as those who put it more tactfully say, we have a strong bent toward "authenticity." Hence, I fear, the polls may never reflect well on us.

Like it or not, it is hard to deny that the "authenticity" factor has climaxed in our generation. I was born in 1978—the same year that First Lady Betty Ford wrote a public statement announcing she was checking into the Long Beach Naval Hospital's rehab center after overmedicating herself. At the time, not everyone thought it was appropriate for the first lady to expose her flaws to the nation. As White House reporter Helen Thomas put it, "To be honest about an addiction problem took a lot of courage. People do not want to be considered any other way than perfect, especially first ladies."

Mrs. Ford also was among the first of America's elite to talk about breast cancer and premarital sex with the cameras rolling. And not only did she broach these touchy subjects, she occasionally offered different views than her husband's (which prompted controversy over the appropriate role of the first lady). I guess it's easy to see why Robert Barrett, an aide to President Ford, told the *New York Times* in 1978: "We've never had too much success in keeping Mrs. Ford's mouth shut."[2]

In the eighteen years that followed Mrs. Ford's admission to Long Beach Naval Hospital, the world grew increasingly comfortable with authenticity. By the time I was old enough to vote in 1996, I could browse a 445-page online report about the extramarital affair of incumbent candidate President William Jefferson Clinton.

Even then, I never realized how raw the world had become. Not until I read this newsflash: After Clinton's report was posted on the House of Representatives website, visitors started streaming in to the tune of three million hits per hour (66,000 hits per hour was normal).[3] The online report was so popular, it prompted Jay Leno to quip, "I'll bet Clinton's glad he put a computer in every classroom."

President Clinton's intern mishaps were not the only executive branch blunders that made public airwaves. Comedians from

David Letterman to the cast of *Saturday Night Live* found easy targets in everything from Vice President Dan Quayle's spelling ability to President George W. Bush's speaking slipups. Although people had probably long noticed the inadequacies of politicians, the world we grew up in was willing to make fun of their flaws out loud.

Of course, in the twentysomethings' school days, you didn't have to be a politician to have your private life broadcast for the nation. Thanks to a wide range of talk-show hosts, including Phil Donahue, Jenny Jones, Geraldo, Oprah, Ricki Lake, and Montel Williams, viewers could look on as "average" citizens grappled with real-life issues, from reuniting with lost relatives to confronting unfaithful lovers. "By the summer of 1993 the television page of *USA Today* listed seventeen talk shows and local papers as many as twenty-seven."[4]

Perhaps one of the rawest talk show stories hails from Springerland. The host? Jerry Springer, a Cincinnati city councilman who resigned in 1971 after police discovered a check he had written to a prostitute. After waiting only one year, Springer ran for city council again and was reelected. Two years later, Springer became mayor of Cincinnati at age thirty-three. After an unsuccessful attempt at winning the Ohio governorship, Springer was hired as a political reporter for NBC's Cincinnati affiliate and within two years was their Emmy award-winning top news anchor. This success likely led to his talk show, *The Jerry Springer Show*, which first aired in 1991, and would proceed to gain him a reputation as the nation's smuttiest talk show host.[5]

Perhaps it was talk shows like Springer's that led to the authenticity generation's recent phenomenon—reality TV. Just when the world thought TV couldn't get any more transparent, surveillance crews began tailing people and providing fly-on-the-wall views into everyday human routines (although when it came to the likes of Ozzy Osbourne and Jessica Simpson, it wasn't quite human life as usual).

In March 1989, *COPS* debuted. The plot? There really wasn't one. Cameras followed on-duty police officers as they responded to speeding violations and domestic violence disputes. Soon after came MTV's *The Real World*, which became one of the most popular and long lasting reality shows to date. In 2002, *Big Brother* premiered in Europe and *Survivor* hit the US. From there, reality television exploded.

The Real World, to expand on one example, topped expressions of authenticity by inserting seven young people in a New York City loft and rolling the cameras as they locked lips, slammed doors, and broke down in tears. In thirteen episodes, Andre, Becky, Eric, Heather, Julie, Kevin, and Norman launched a trend that would continue for sixteen seasons of volatile disagreements, steamy makeout sessions, and drunken escapades to date.

Today, as I write this letter, you can find a list of 324 US-based reality shows, along with two Canadian-based, three Australian-based, and twenty-eight UK-based programs at *www.realitytv links.com*.

Is it any surprise that a world exposed to this level of everyday drama expects its church to feel real and maybe sometimes a little bit raw as well?

I was reminded of how this authenticity lens applies to the church when I interacted with Gregg Farah, pastor of Mosaic Manhattan in New York City. Mosaic's church, which was planted in March 2003, is largely made up of twenty- to fortysomething professionals, artists, and students.

When I asked Gregg what kind of initiatives Mosaic used to attract such a dominantly young crowd, unsurprisingly he answered, "I don't think there's been any significant initiative we've pursued. We've simply attempted to honestly and authentically listen and communicate."

Gregg observes that authenticity is one of the "grids" many people today use to view relationships. Questions he hears them asking are, "Can I trust you?" "Are you trustworthy enough that I can be authentic?" and "Will you respond to me in a consistent way?" If the answer is yes, Gregg notes, "the relationship progresses."

Of course, on the other hand, when there is a lack of authenticity, relationships come to a screeching halt.

I can vouch for this firsthand. There is very little in this world that stretches my patience more than apparent inauthenticity in the church.

One of the most memorable offenses to stick in my mind unfolded like this: It was Sunday morning. The speaker on the church's stage smiled a fit-for-a-toothpaste-commercial grin while kicking off the service with a noticeably upbeat intro. "I tell you what," Speaker Man beamed, "I feel so lucky to be part of this church. When I talk to other Christians who live hours away from here, they always tell me how jealous they are that I go here."

I'll spare you the gory details of the self-applause, Church. But know that by the time Speaker Man had finished, he had done everything but pass out pom-poms to the worship team to convince his audience that their local congregation was God's gift to the universe.

In fact, if you heard Speaker Man's spiel, you might even think he rehearsed it ahead of time.

He probably did.

While hanging out in the lobby after the first Sunday service to talk with some people in the church hallway, I heard the second service ramping up just like the first. It started—almost word for word—the exact same way. "All my friends are jealous that I go here ..."

The person I was talking to winced as the words slipped out through the auditorium doors. Smirking, she joked, "If I had an Oscar on hand, I swear I would walk up there and interrupt the service to hand it to him." Then she released a long, hard sigh. "I hate to break it to them, but people aren't exactly busting down the doors to get in right now."

I sighed right along with her.

Perhaps our level of repulsion was a bit dramatic, but it wasn't completely unfounded. The previous few weeks had been marked by painful transition and relational fallout that was noticeable well outside of the twentysomething arena. While every church has its lows, several older members sadly confessed that this particular drama surpassed normal church dysfunction. We were spelunking in the Mariana Trench of congregational issues.

One had to guess the preplanned pep talk was related to recent events.

Focus on the guy on stage, listen to his booming radio voice, and stare into his bright white teeth. *Our church is still good. Just don't look behind the curtain.*

And he was right. The church *was* still good. But so good everyone else was jealous? Well, maybe not on that particular day. Why not acknowledge the hurt instead of sweeping things under the carpet?

Any way you slice it, twentysomethings have hypersensitive internal sensors when it comes to authenticity. Margaret Feinberg advises churches who *don't* want to connect with our generation:

> Be fake. Don't be yourself. Be someone else all the time. Put on a show. Dress in clothes that really aren't your style, simply because they're hip. Buy the latest gadgets (even though you'll never use them) so you can say you own one. And most importantly, use the latest teenage language. Since most of the twentysomethings in your group don't even know teen talk, you'll sound like you're really "in." Make it obvious that you really want to be cool in everything you do more than you want to be like Jesus. This will help ensure the twentysomethings hungering for authentic relationships and faith go somewhere else.[6]

Thanks to Margaret, you might be wondering what *are* some of the "inauthenticities" that might make twentysomethings — and others — "go elsewhere."

Other church-related authenticity breakdowns reported by twentysomethings include:

- Churches that pressure participants to raise their hands, engage in clap offerings, or offer other preplanned responses throughout the services. (We don't mind that the option is mentioned, but don't plague us about it, please. Sometimes we are engaging God differently—but no less actively—than the people on stage.)
- Churches whose teams try to overpolish the worship services. (We like a few good song sets and quality speakers, but we don't like to see people sweating bullets over a slightly squeaky microphone or a typo on the big screen.)
- Churches that come down hard on certain sins, but allow other ones to run rampant ... even in their own lives. (When was the last time we had a heart-to-heart about Deacon Donutlover's gut, for example?)
- Churches that inflate attendance numbers or take every opportunity to toss them out. Same goes for bragging about other church "achievements." (We are glad you have something to celebrate, but there are still times when a little old-school "to God be the glory" might be in order.)
- Churches that are heavy on secrecy. (It is specifically when questions are discouraged that people feel a need to ask the most questions.)
- Churches whose leaders pretend to get along on stage— singing and smiling at each other as the service unfolds —only to boldly gossip about each other when the spotlight goes down. (Often the teams that truly excel are teams that can get along on *and* off the field.)
- Churches whose onstage dress code seems to keep designer clothing stores in business. (When Abercrombie starts sending you endorsement checks, it might be time for a change ... of clothes.)
- Churches that go overboard on the "experiential" or "high-tech" factor. (Contrary to popular belief, if the fire

department shows up for weekly false alarms, that might be a sign you have a few too many candles on stage ... no matter how "cool" they are.)

- Churches that are obsessed with being on top of the "latest"—whether it be technology, music, books, or lingo. (While the cutting edge may *seem* cool, our parents taught us to be careful around sharp blades.)

Authenticity is not just about what goes on in-house though. The church's inability to "be real" can also shorten its evangelical arm reach.

For instance, it's difficult to disciple people when your role in their lives has an expiration date.

Here's a perfect example of what I mean by that: While tutoring at a homeless shelter one afternoon, one of our fourth graders abruptly refused to finish his homework.

"Boomer, what's going on?" I straddled the metal folding chair next to his.

"Nothing. I ain't doin' it," he replied, his words heavy with an anger that didn't correspond with math problems or any other issues children his age normally face.

"Okay, let's just try," I suggested. "You go ahead and read this next one to me." I pointed to one of the remaining four story problems.

Boomer shook his head.

"Come on. I'll help you," I coaxed. "We'll read it together."

Reluctantly, Boomer leaned forward and rested his forehead against his hand. Peering down at the paper, he began stumbling through the words, his voice barely audible as I read aloud.

In seconds, the problem was obvious.

Boomer was in fourth grade, but he couldn't read ... at all.

I spent the rest of the evening making flashcards. Boomer and I worked on them for weeks. Well, for two weeks, that is. It would've been longer, but one afternoon when I showed up for tutoring, a shelter staff member informed me that Boomer was gone.

"His mom just left. Took the kids with her," she said simply, as if these unexplained exits were half-expected.

They were.

I thought about Boomer the rest of the night. I thought about more than just the flashcards he left behind or how he'd feel entering fifth grade still not knowing how to read. I wondered instead about Boomer's personal development, about whether he'd have many opportunities to be spiritually mentored as he grew up.

In two short weeks, I—an award-winning representative of the Super Church—hadn't even been able to teach Boomer to read, let alone make a dent in his spiritual formation.

I hadn't been able to cast a strong enough vision to compete with the gang Boomer knew he would join as soon as he turned fourteen. I hadn't been able to offer vocational training or life skills that would rival the lure and excitement of luxury cars, expensive clothes, and women that gang money could buy. And I hadn't been able to convince Boomer that if he pursued the right goals, he really might live past eighteen without ending up in jail—an outcome he already deemed impossible.

In those moments of reflection, some of my earlier suspicions were confirmed. Sunday school and junior church had not taught me all the skills necessary to invite Boomer, and other people unlike me, into real relationship with Christ or his church. When it came to Jesus, I realized, I barely knew how to be authentic.

See, Boomer didn't fit neatly into the Evangelism 101 curriculum I'd been raised on. Neither did a lot of other people I encountered in America's cities.

I could say the Romans Road with my eyes closed and my hands tied behind my back. I could pass out a hundred tracts faster than you could shuffle a deck of cards. I had been delivering the Sinner's Prayer to my Cabbage Patches for years. I had WWJD bracelets in every color of the rainbow, a purity ring on each hand, a bona fide Gideon's Bible in my coat pocket, and a well-rehearsed plan of salvation I could present in sixty seconds flat.

Even with all these skills, when I ran into people like Boomer and his mother, the idea of building lifelong friendships rarely if ever even crossed my mind. When I interacted with them, I often shifted into the gear the church had taught me to operate in: "missions project mode."

I was operating in missions mode, for instance, while tutoring at the shelter.

By evangelism standards, I was not only doing my tutoring job, but I was going *above and beyond* what was required of me by teaching Boomer to read after hours.

And let's not forget my other previously unmentioned low-flying evangelical contributions. For instance, I cleverly worked "If I Were a Butterfly" and other Christian kids' songs into the activities portion of the tutoring sessions. I let the kids color with *my* magic markers. In fact, out of the generosity of my heart, I flat out gave them my $1.99 pack of washable Crayolas. (That's right, no strings attached!) I even stayed afterward to help stack chairs and wash tables.

Every day, I walked into the shelter cafeteria knowing exactly what my job was. And every day, I walked out feeling satisfied that my outreach to-do list was completed.

Feel-good fix? Check.

Another smiley face sticker fixed next to my name on heaven's good deeds chart? Check.

One more spiritual merit badge to wear with my choir robe? Check.

But wait, there's more. In a moment of decision that seemed to blow the tent off most Sunday-evening revivals, I vowed to do similar outreach projects for *life*.

I intended to blow my measly paychecks on extra mittens for the annual winter clothing drive. I intended to sponsor three—count them, three—children for the Christmas Angel Tree campaign. *And*, to add a little spit polish to my halo, I was going to volunteer to deliver Thanksgiving turkeys while wearing the brightest, boldest, most compelling Christian T-shirt I could find.

I was going to be a two-mile walker, a tunic-and-cloak giver, a slapped-cheek turner. Introduce me to the hungry and I was going to feed them. Point me to the prisoners and I was going to visit them. Show me the drinking fountain and I was going to serve one mean glass of water in Jesus' name.

My life was going to be the testimony old women who dominated praise-and-prayer-request-time lived to share.

But even those intentions fell short.

Discipling Boomer was not a stop-drop-and-roll-him-to-the-altar type of affair. It was a slow-dripping, life-on-life witness that required ongoing, spiritually nurturing relationship.

And I, the former captain of fifth-grade Bible quizzing, had rarely been drilled in creating and maintaining real-life relationship with those unlike myself. Come to think about it, I'm not sure most other people in my church were either.

In general, when a church responded to someone in need—whether it be a church lifer or someone like Boomer—I often saw them turn to an age-old premise: Every need can be answered by the right church program.

This was part of my logic too.

I have to admit, when I ran into many of the city's needy, my church-trained mind flew into overdrive: *Okay, all we need to do is find some churches who have programs to serve their local populations. Surely, one of these steeple-clad places has a job-training program, a housing ministry, a drug rehab clinic. Something to penetrate the difficulty of these people's lives with the hope of Jesus.*

But a lot of times, people need a support system more than they need programs, they need love more than they need curriculum, and they need real-life friends more than they need another once-a-week discussion group.

In all my attempts to help people with some quick-fix outreach initiative or by getting them onto your rosters, Church, the most legitimate thing my efforts turned up was an I'm-gonna-be-sick feeling in the pit of my stomach. I was saddened by my own inauthenticity and the inauthenticity of my church.

And I mean *truly* saddened.

Saddened that I had sunk so much of myself, so much of my life, my energy, my time, and my resources into a very specific model of church ... only to back up and wonder if I had invested everything-I-had-and-then-some in an inauthentic church model.

Or, maybe it wasn't even so much an *inauthentic* model.

Maybe I just wasn't convinced it was the *most authentic* model. To put it bluntly, there are moments when I wonder whether the talking-head-driven, program-centered, building-focused, mission-project-heavy version is the best expression of church that we are capable of producing.

I hate and yet, at the same time, I love the possibility that our existing church models may not necessarily be God's final models.

On one hand, this possibility generates an internal fear response — the instinctive desire to protect my pride and reassure myself that my own mode of church has been wisely chosen and doesn't need improvement. But on the other hand, the possibility deepens me; it allows me to find a more humble and genuine place before a God who, I think, still shapes plans for his church that are superior to mine. Plans that, if they existed, would be worth seeking.

In fact, if I were wise, I think I would seek God's possibilities more often. Every day, if I could stand it. I would want to live every minute — and I would want every believer to live every minute — with these questions imprinted on our hearts: *Can we live church, can we be church, can we bring church to expression in a way that tops the world's current definitions of "church"? Could we somehow generate a collective of believers that is even more compelling, even more complete, even more sincere at inviting people to align themselves with God?*

Part of my own questioning has led me to desire a more authentic church: a congregation that is sincere both in its presentation to and relationship with its people.

Of course, like many ideals, this one starts out kind of blurry. After all, what exactly *is* an authentic church? It's not like you can just flip to the glossary in the back of your Bible and memorize the definition.

In fact, at one level, it is illogical to try to define an authentic church because the second you declare one particular set of traits to be "authentic," you have forced everyone to try to copy your ideas—which is *in*authentic!

The process of becoming more authentic, like the process of becoming more like Christ, is a journey. In fact, I'll take it one step further. It *has* to be a journey. Authenticity is not a trait you put on overnight. It can't ever be a tag like "relevant" or "emergent" or even "seeker" or "purpose-driven." Churches can't pay an association fee or read a certain book in order to be listed on some online directory of "authentic churches." Authenticity doesn't work that way.

We as individuals—people who *are* the church and who influence local congregations—must commit ourselves to seeking out and taking advantage of opportunities to truly, nonprogrammatically live our faith every day. Gradually, as we exercise authenticity, we will develop eyes and ears and words that allow us to nurture spirituality through authenticity.

As *we* learn authenticity, the church will learn authenticity. And as the *church* learns authenticity, I can only hope, the world will connect with our message.

This said, of course, I don't have a scripted formula for churches who desire to be authentic. All I have is a fragmented list of observations I have made while trying to be spiritually authentic in my own sphere of influence. I can only justify presenting it to you as a list of personal learnings—nothing more.

In order to be authentic, I would be wise to:

- *Allow God to be mysterious sometimes.* Rather than trying to force my hand-selected information about God on others, I have learned to acknowledge that what we are inviting others into is an interactive mystery—some of which I can't fully explain and shouldn't try to, some of which is yet to be solved. I have found that faith is owned and internalized at a far more intense rate when we allow people to explore genuinely, to seek truth and not just our pre-selected answers.

- *Invest more of my energies into keeping my own heart in order.* I find that when I am not centered on God's ideals, such as hope and peace and love, I become more self-serving. I serve more from a desire to affirm my own goodness, to give myself a self-esteem high, than from a desire to truly connect with others. When I interact with others only to build my own self-worth, they can often sense that I am not truly interested in connecting with them, but only carrying out one more task on my spiritual to-do list.

- *Define conversion outside of just a simple repeat-after-me prayer.* All too often converts don't fully understand that the words they repeat in such a prayer are supposed to be *weighty* words. Words that mark an internal shift, an intention to understand and practice a new life philosophy. Words that point to a new alliance, an allegiance to God and his ideals.

  Sadly, I find that when I give potential converts the thirty-second Jesus spiel (to save them from hell) and then release myself of any long-term commitment to spiritually disciple them, they become victims of shallow root syndrome. Human life goes on—cursed as it was before, dysfunctional as it was before, painful as it was before—and this simple sentence, minus the transformation that comes from internalizing God's truth over the long haul, sets them up for spiritual failure. Their roots do not go down deep enough; their roots don't know how to find or drink water.

- *Accept that even when people choose a different path than I would choose for them, they are exercising their God-given right to do so.* Rather than panicking or excessively interfering with their choices, I've learned that God can reveal himself just as well through any painful consequences they experience as he can in the noonday sun. Mistakes are not necessarily dead ends, they are often expressways to enlightenment. In releasing some of the control factor to God, I demonstrate that I *authentically* believe that God is capable of revealing himself and transforming lives without me overseeing every step of the process.

- *Realize that my best witness is my most natural one.* Many of us want to overprepare ourselves so we can articulately and convincingly explain the salvation plan to others. We want to feel intellectually strong enough to outdebate and outwit any person who is resistant to the faith. But, in my experiences, this rehearsed style of evangelism often seems to run contrary to what actually draws people to God. Most people in my life are only marginally influenced by my memorized salvation verbiage. Quite the opposite, I win or lose most debates about the reality of God based on whether or not God is reflected in my reality. My best evangelism is prolonged life-on-life contact.

- *Take advantage of natural, routine opportunities to disciple others, rather than investing a disproportionate amount of time and energy into church-orchestrated programs.* I wonder about the value of picking twelve random people to be my "small group" one hour a week versus the value of discipling and inspiring the twelve not-so-random people who are in my life the 167 hours I am not in church.

- *Disciple others broadly, so that they are not just equipped to serve in my specific church's programs, but can recognize and respond to God's movement in their lives no matter what the context.* That way, no matter what they do—whether they attend my church, change churches, or stop going to church altogether—they would know how to nurture spiritual support and accountability systems.

- *Invite people into a network of spiritual friendships, rather than just an organization* (although an organization *can* facilitate a network of spiritual friendships, this is not always the case). A person can easily miss the point of a sixty-minute service, but it is much more difficult to miss the sense of "kingdom here" that is experienced when surrounded by a group of like-minded Christ-followers who are living out God's ideals in close proximity to each other.

- *Admit my own shortcomings more quickly and more often.* Of all the people who have shared disillusioning church experiences with me, the great majority were disillusioned because someone who claimed to represent God failed to represent God's ideals in a particular situation. While part of the solution is, of course, to represent God *better*, an equally crucial part is being willing to acknowledge when our own behavior strays from our intentions.

    Just this year, while teaching my high school students, I took up a new practice: following my apologies with one simple statement, "That is not who I want to be." If I speak too harshly or hastily to a student, I try to immediately retrace my steps. "I am sorry for being short with you. That is not who I want to be." By doing this, I believe I reinforce what type of behavior belongs in a healthy Christian life and I am admitting that certain behaviors have no place in one. This practice with my students has single-handedly increased my credibility beyond anything else I have ever done.

- *Forgive more quickly and more often.* When church people judge others too harshly, we create a climate of spiritual perfectionism in which people are afraid to be honest about barriers to their own spiritual growth. I have found that forgiveness—like salvation—must also extend past a simple exchange of words. Forgiveness is an attitude that implies an internal understanding that we are no better than anyone else around us. Forgiveness infers that we will not only verbally forgive, we won't hold others' failures against them.

- *Be willing to closely examine church programs I advocate.* I find that it is valuable to ask myself: does participating in this program inspire people to seek God more or does it motivate them to pursue success within the church system? I can't afford to *not* know the difference.

Of course, idealist-to-a-fault twentysomethings like myself must acknowledge that authenticity is a two-way street. My generation has a role to play in shaping the solutions we long for.

Author and columnist Andy Crouch suggests part of that role is patience.

To make this point, Crouch recalls his younger days when denim jeans had to be washed over and over and over again in order to yield a more comfortable fit. (Very young readers might not know this because, as Crouch points out, Levi's eventually got smart and started selling jeans that were already prewashed or as it was more popularly termed "stonewashed.")

"I've been thinking about the days of board-like denim as I hear people describe their longing for an 'authentic' church," he writes. "*Authenticity* is the watchword of a generation that is suspicious of squeaky-clean, franchise Christianity. Last month I spoke at a young, thriving church that describes itself as 'real church for real people.' I could understand the appeal of that phrase. Church, and church people, can often seem unreal."

However, Crouch notes that such critiques of the church can reflect impatience.

Our attitude toward church is much like our approach to denim. "We'd like our church authentic, and we'd like it authentic when we first put it on," Crouch observes.[7]

Fair enough, Mr. Crouch.

We—or at least, I—see your point. And I am more than happy to pen patience into a top priority spot on my to-do list ... that is, as long as you'll let me and a few other twentysomethings stow some stones in the church's washing machine.

I can't help thinking there's gotta be a way to get the church in more comfortable condition before people put it on.

Discussion Questions

1. Do you think that people are tempted to lie about church attendance? Why?
2. Do you think the stigma attached to "not attending" church has changed over time?
3. Why do you think reality TV has become so popular?
4. Do certain parts of church strike you as fake? If so, which ones?
5. What kind of strengths and weaknesses might come along with a desire for authenticity?
6. Can you relate to the author's story about her interactions with Boomer? Have you ever participated in a missions project that seemed more "task driven" than relationally authentic?
7. What do you think churches could do to ensure their programs do not become more important than personal relationships?

Key Observation

Because world media grows increasingly authentic,
an image-managed church can seem fake
and dishonest by contrast.

Sketches in Progress

Dear Church,

A few years ago I attended a Christian conference that drew participants from all over the world. One group of attenders that was particularly interesting to me had traveled from a remote part of Africa to visit the United States for the first time.

Early in the conference, a cameraman filmed the group as they entered the huge auditorium. As everyone applauded their welcome, the camera zoomed in on the group who smiled broadly and, rightly so, looked slightly overwhelmed at the social frenzy.

Periodically, throughout the event, I would catch a glimpse of the African group. Every time I saw them, they seemed understandably mesmerized—completely fixated on all the elements of their surroundings. They seemed to be forcing themselves into constant-alert mode—drinking in every detail of their context—as if allowing themselves to even blink, they might miss something important. You could see an unusual sense of awe in their faces—not like the awe of being surprised in one instant, but a consistent sense of amazement like children who were visiting an enormous toy store for the first time. Every section, every aisle, every shelf held something new, something they couldn't wait to see and touch and explore.

I couldn't resist trying to guess the thoughts behind the group's sometimes puzzled reactions. I imagined their village—shown in an earlier slide show—and their more familiar church setting, housed in a facility much more low-tech than the arena they found themselves in. I couldn't help wondering if the look on their faces—as they took in the bright lights and speakers and video footage—was accompanied by the question, "*This* is church?" Might they be trying to comprehend how Acts 2 and the epistles had somehow translated into an enormous complex that hosted weekend events from a stage that would rival a U2 performance.

In fact, I reflected, I wonder if good old Luke and the famed apostle Paul would be doing just as many double takes as these African guests. Would Peter and the other leaders of the early New Testament church be sitting at this conference pondering, "How did the church end up becoming like this?"

Apparently, I am not the only one who has wondered such thoughts.

According to Dan Kimball, author of *The Emerging Church*, "There is a rising restlessness that perhaps what most are experiencing in their churches does not match what they are reading in the New Testament about what 'church' was."[1]

I agree with Dan. And I think it's safe to say that twenty-somethings are among the restless. I'm afraid we have been groomed to be critical thinkers who question absolutely everything … including the church.

For some of this tendency, you can perhaps credit my parents' generation. Following on the heels of Great Depression veterans, they largely hit their rite of passage in the late sixties and early seventies. Some who were nicknamed "hippies" or "flower children" birthed a distinctive thread of American culture that many still imitate today (à la *That '70s Show* and the return of the Beetle). Some of their trademarks included—among other things—long hairstyles for men, bright fabrics with crazy patterns, rock and roll, tie-dye, and Volkswagen buses. All stylistic choices, which seemed to say, "We are going to embrace what we like, even if it flies in the face of tradition." (Even my dad, Mr. Southern Baptist Church Planter himself, had a rebelliously long hairstyle.)

Some in that generation adopted the mantra "make love not war," inviting experimentation with marijuana and sex, which probably seemed like attractive alternatives to their parents' stories about World War II ... and even more so, their own generation's war in Vietnam.

Speaking of the war, the children of the sixties and seventies gained their political voice early. They became comfortable with expressing their ideals, singing and speaking freely about what they thought the world should be and about how they thought world powers should operate. Of course, they produced more than just some surviving recordings of Woodstock. Thanks to leaders like Martin Luther King Jr. and John F. Kennedy, our parents overturned life as it was and ushered in a new era of equal rights.

The learnings of the sixties and seventies, then, became our parents' platform for raising children. And so, they encouraged us to be free thinkers, telling us that we lived in a free country where the draft could be challenged and no one had the right to tell us what to do with our lives.

(A great example of this: I helped my high school senior class lead a cafeteria boycott. And my mom was one of many mothers who helped provide alternative sources of food for the entire school.)

We were given permission to question the status quo ... if not outright encouraged to do so. Not only were we *not* forced to accept social norms, but we were in some ways groomed to be suspicious of them.

Standing up to authority rarely resulted in the whiplashings of the past. Parents sometimes even seemed to side with their children over traditional authority figures. Suddenly when teachers called home to let Dad and Mom know that Junior misbehaved, some parents blew up at the teacher and defended their children. (Oh, to be so lucky to be raised in such a household!)

Some might say that my generation grew too quickly to question authority and excuse ourselves from blame. And, admittedly, our rights-heavy lifestyle was a philosophy that—when abused—backfired. Hence, our court systems saw isolated cases in which children sued their parents, asking the judge to let them divorce their natural families!

Given our background, it is not especially shocking to see twentysomethings enter adulthood with a penchant for dissecting society's institutions. I have to admit, I'm no exception to the rule. I have ample doubt as to whether the edition of church I inherited is an accurate expression of God's original intentions.

It seems to me that, when it comes to church, people are born with a blank canvas. A clean slate. Unsure of what church is meant to be, what it means to anyone else, or what it will come to mean to them.

From day one on, though, other people gradually help us fill up our canvas. The first line, our first construct for understanding what church is, is probably most often drawn by our parents.

Perhaps, at three or four years old, we overhear Mom say in passing "that church puts on the most spectacular Easter services." Immediately, this piece of information — this line — becomes our first vague inkling of what church might be. *Churches put on services. Churches celebrate Easter.*

A few years after, we coast past a building while enjoying a routine bike ride with friends. We only know the building is a church because it has a sign out front which clearly labels it "Bethany Christian Church." Instantly, another line is drawn in our minds. Another construct is formed: *The church has a building.* Or maybe even, *The church is a building.*

Some time later, as we are casually flipping through the Yellow Pages we spot some additional information. "Sunday 10 a.m. worship service," one ad of many reads. And in go more lines. *People worship something at church. People go to church on Sundays.* And, thanks to the numerous ads, *There is more than one church.*

These lines, at least at a basic level, are required for understanding the concept of church. Whether metaphoric or literal, they are necessary to grasp the meaning the church brings to an otherwise blank universe.

We sketch out names to mark our local church's geographic meeting places, buildings to define space that is available for mission, and doctrines to outline belief systems.

Helping people develop these constructs for understanding you is a beautiful opportunity, Church, but it is also a dangerous one.

As we sketch a line here and add a line there, tossing out bits of information about "what church is," we can unintentionally draw a picture that does not represent God's real intentions for you.

Unfortunately, some of us may draw lines like there's no tomorrow. One, two, ten, twenty. We get line happy. Obsessed, maybe, with drawing lines, with laying down constructs, with adding onto the definition of church.

Small groups, children's ministries, hospitality teams, greeters, ushers, membership, leadership, fellowship, outreach, missions, sermon series, devotionals, doctrines ... before long, we end up with so many lines even *we* can't even keep track of all the ones we've drawn.

Somewhere in our jumbled evolving sketch, we have to acknowledge (if we are honest) that we may have adopted some unnecessary lines. Some misleading lines. Even some hurtful ones.

The following list denotes some of the lines the disillusioned may tend to question—some of the lines that those I have spoken with are not sure belong in our definition or impressions of church. Some of these, you will see, should not be thrown out altogether. They may be needed or beneficial to our understanding but perhaps could stand a little artistic tweaking. Maybe when they were drawn they were slightly crooked or off center.

The Attendance Line

The disillusioned are likely to question whether attendance or even membership in a local church is a trustworthy indicator of a person's allegiance to Christ. Like many of you, we have noted that a person's behavior during one sixty-minute time slot is not always reliable evidence of alignment with God's values. We are concerned about worldviews that measure a person's commitment or loyalty to Christ's cause by how long or how often he or she has attended church. Similarly, we don't think falling away from church always means someone is falling away from God. (We do not deny that regular and long-term church attendance can spur on spiritual growth, but there is enough variation in the results that it seems unwise to use this as our only barometer.)

The Infrastructure Line

In addition, the disillusioned may question practices that identify leadership caliber by how much time or energy a person contributes to maintaining the church's infrastructure. Let's say, for example, that person A logs a thousand hours on the church's greeter team while person B sinks a thousand hours into coaching soccer teams in the community. Both of them could be all-star witnesses for Christ who maximize their face time building deep spiritual relationships with others. Yet we ask: supposing both of them are on target for Christ, which post is more likely to be applauded or commissioned by their local church? The answer to this question, I would suggest, is why we have more Christians on the greeter team than we have on the soccer fields.

The Numbers Line

Churches often claim that they are not in the "numbers" business—that church ministry is not about growing in size, but about growing people's souls. We must acknowledge, though, that this doesn't entirely prevent us from working attendance numbers into the bulletin or onstage announcements. Yes, numbers *can* be an indication of God's movement or of effective discipleship. And knowing numbers are increasing makes us feel as though we are doing our job well.

However, the disillusioned often raise eyebrows at frequent or exaggerated claims of expansion. Spiritual growth, we note, is not necessarily synonymous with numeric growth. Rather, we're wary of trends that transform churches into instant hot spots. After all, an accident on the side of the road or a burning building can create a crowd. Sadly, attracting a following doesn't necessarily prove spiritual validity; sometimes it just indicates the presence of gawkers.

The Programming Line

The disillusioned are sometimes hesitant to embrace programming techniques employed to gain our attention. Although services deemed "artistic," "participatory," or "relevant" may genuinely strike the young as cool, we recognize that not everything that is cool has spiritual payoff. Services that play too much to our entertainment or to social trends can feel like commercialized ploys to those of us who pride ourselves on being critical thinkers.

The Applause Line

While attracting media attention may be a sign that God's favor rests on a local church, it may also reflect that the pastor knows the reporter or news anchor. We worry that churches who do edgy or experimental things to create curiosity or gain public attention may eventually be tempted to make decisions according to what creates the biggest splash. Thanks to CNN, MSNBC, and other round-the-clock news shows, we know that some reporters are willing to follow any big bang—be it a miracle or a train wreck. Their need to fill up a sixty-minute news slot doesn't necessarily equal God's stamp of approval on a local congregation.

The Discipleship Line

Like me, some of the disillusioned have learned a hard lesson. Regular interactions with church leaders during childhood do not constitute discipleship. We know this because too many of our childhood peers who warmed the pews never gained the spiritual equipment necessary to derive purpose or boundaries for healthy adult living. In our eyes, then, inviting people to church is not the same as being willing to disciple them. Similarly, getting them to attend does not mean they now know Jesus. And getting them to stay does not mean they are growing closer to God.

The Leadership Line

Many of the disillusioned are waiting for a cause to grab onto, yet we may resist alignment with the church for fear that churches want their leaders to trade in their identities for a "churchier" version of themselves (please note: I am *not* protesting churches aiming at a more Christlike version of ourselves). My generation's ideas about what a leader should look like are as diverse as our world. Many of us insist, then, that followers of Christ were created with a diverse heritage and conditioned by diverse experiences that should not, upon discipleship, be ironed out into one seamless expression of what it means to be Christian. We can't all be articulate, middle-class, college-educated, Gap-wearing, small-group leaders. And if we were, who would be in relationship with world citizens who will never attend a small group or shop at Gap?

The Evangelism Line

Engle scalelike models, developed by respected thinkers like Dr. James Engle, can be useful tools for observing a person's spiritual conversion. However, any formulaic plan that insists on one common starting point and outlines specific step-by-step progression often strikes us as too limiting. Engle, for example, suggests people move from awareness of the supernatural to interest in Christianity to understanding the gospel and so on. Many in my generation diverge from formulas like these. The majority of them, for example, seem to be aware and even interested in Christianity long before they ever realize there is anything "supernatural" about it. We expect there are other variances within our generation and within other age groups that make linear conversion paths like this a bit impractical.

The Success Line

Some of the disillusioned have encountered church leaders who hope for a very specific end product—not only spiritual disciples, but disciples who are advancing themselves economically, socially, and educationally. Aside from congregations that preach generous versions of the prosperity gospel, I have met several peers who have been "spiritually" counseled and even pressured to pursue higher-level education and jobs within their companies. There is nothing wrong with "whatever you do, do it heartily as unto the Lord." However, we don't think that everyone belongs in administrative or management offices. If this were God's aim, don't you think it would seem a bit shortsighted for him not to have anyone down on the assembly lines to build relationships with the people there? People in different occupations or social classes are needed to reach people who may never come in contact with CEO-style Christians.

The Image Management Line

Although I was raised to strive toward blamelessness and still try to be above reproach in my own behavior, I—like many of the disillusioned—have seen some churches go overboard in pushing spiritual perfectionism. Leaders who have to manufacture a near-faultless image to attract people to their churches often feel like they must then maintain the image so people will stay. And as I mentioned in my previous letter about authenticity, attempts at image management often lead to problems. Camouflaging your flaws is like pretending your car never needs an oil change ... an act you will eventually have to maintain all the way to the mechanic.

The Superhero Line

As I noted back in my first letter, as a college kid I was completely enamored by the idea that the church was the "hope of the world." I internalized this claim so deeply that I subconsciously began drawing hope from the organization itself. As follows, I came to believe that I—as a member of the church—could be a reliable source of hope as well. These days, I still believe that people can encounter hope in the church, but my idealistic view of the church has now been forcibly refined through real-life encounters with people who have not gleaned hope from their sometimes hurtful run-ins with the church.

« »

For some of my peers and other disillusioned Christians, the aforementioned lines are just the warm-up. We may continue the scrutiny, effectively X-raying every line in the whole church package. We question, for example, how many of the following constructs—or lines—are necessary to the definition of church?

- An artistic facility
- A twenty-to-thirty-minute sermon
- A passed-around offering
- Baptistries
- Serving refreshments in the lobby
- High-tech lighting
- Coffeehouses or other alternative locations
- Steeples
- Digital screens
- High ceilings
- Guitars and saxes
- The American or Christian flags
- Seminaries
- Pulpits
- Stages
- Pews and/or rows/circles of chairs
- Choirs and/or worship teams
- Praying to close a service
- A 9:30 or 11:00 a.m. Sunday time slot
- Stained-glass windows
- A Communion table with an open Bible
- Stereo sound systems
- Large wooden crosses
- Pianos and organs
- Announcements
- Visitors' or information table
- Altars
- A dress code

- Denominations
- Membership
- Bulletins
- Websites
- A one-hour service
- A video projector
- Individual children's classes divided by grade
- Candles
- A constant supply of Christian literature

- Nondenominations
- Clap offerings
- Mass email lists
- Altar calls
- A worship leader
- Small groups
- The ability to perform weddings
- Nonprofits
- The ability to perform funerals

In identifying all these lines, I should offer a word of caution. As twentysomethings in particular evaluate our definitions of church, we should avoid simplistic game plans that seek only to delete the lines that don't go over well in our generation. We want to do more than just toss out previous lines (organs, fellowship halls, and denominational curriculum, for example) only to draw a "new" set of equivalent lines in their place (guitars, gymnasiums, and hosts of books churned out by the Christian publishing industry).

It may be wiser, then, to only temporarily suspend old lines that have contributed to our previous definitions of you, Church. By doing this, we can get back to that clean canvas and attempt to envision the number and shapes of lines that God himself put into place when instituting his church.

Of course, the natural place to start looking for God's original artistry seems to be the Bible.

We first catch the word *church* thrown out in Jesus' conversation with Peter: "I will build my church, and the gates of death [Hades or hell in other translations] will not overcome it" (Matthew 16:18). And with this sentence we get our first inkling of what church is: *The church is something Jesus builds, something that belongs to him, something that will prevail against evil.*

The more we read, the more our picture of the church expands. We note, for instance, that churches sprouted up in Judea,

Galilee, Samaria, Antioch, Syria, Cilicia, Caesarea, Ephesus, Galatia, and Thessalonia among other places (Acts 9:31; 15:23, 41; 18:22; 20:17; Galatians 1:2; 1 Thessalonians 1:1). Thus, another line falls into place: *More than one group of people can be called church.*

As we flip through Acts, we discover that before Saul became the great apostle Paul, he was bent on destroying the church. But a detail threaded through all the mayhem catches our eye. Paul wasn't demolishing the church by torching buildings. He was taking out the church by dragging off *people* (Acts 8:3). A chapter later, we see the same insinuation (9:1 – 2). Barnabas and Saul are said to meet with the church — note: meet *with* it, not *at* it (11:26). Similarly, we see, the word *church* sometimes points to the believers themselves minus any location of meeting (Matthew 16:18; Ephesians 1:22 – 23). *Huh*, we surmise, *the church seems to be a group of people who follow the teachings of Jesus.*

We could probably spend years absorbed in all the New Testament verses that help us define what church meant to early believers. We can unearth lines that describe church meeting places (Romans 16:5; 1 Corinthians 16:19; Colossians 4:15; Philemon 2), lines that describe church leadership (Acts 6:1 – 6; 14:23; 20:28), lines that describe church activity (Acts 11:26; 13:1), and lines that set Jesus as the premier leader of the church (Ephesians 1:22; 5:23 – 32; Colossians 1:18).

As we take a look at these biblical lines, just as previous generations have done before us, we may even discover that our picture doesn't simply contain extra or unnecessary lines, maybe it also is missing a few lines. Lines that define the church's sense of connectedness, for example, sometimes seem to be missing (or only lightly sketched) in our generation.

The Connection Line

The famed Acts 2 passage, of course, is constantly referenced to show how early believers hung out together regularly: "Every day they continued to meet together in the temple courts. They broke bread in their homes and ate together with glad and sincere hearts, praising God and enjoying the favor of all the people" (vv. 46–47).

This particular community's sense of connection extended past simple social interactions to the wallet. Because these early Christians considered themselves to be of one heart and one mind, "no one claimed that any of their possessions was their own, but they shared everything they had.... There were no needy persons among them. For from time to time those who owned land or houses sold them, brought the money from the sales and put it at the apostles' feet, and it was distributed to anyone who had need" (Acts 4:32–35).

Even more striking than local church connectedness, though, was the sense of connectedness in the more global version of the church.

Apparently, for example, some believers considered themselves to be representatives of churches—plural (2 Corinthians 8:23). Leaders such as Paul felt concern for all churches (2 Corinthians 11:28) and thus spoke for "all the churches of Christ" in Romans 16:16 and for "the churches in the province of Asia" in 1 Corinthians 16:19. When he admonished the church in Corinth, Paul noted that his instructions also were intended for "all those everywhere who call on the name of our Lord Jesus Christ." Eight verses later, he pleaded with his wide range of readers from Corinth and beyond to "be perfectly united in mind and thought" (1 Corinthians 1:2, 10).

Churches were expected to treat believers outside their local community like brothers. The church of Corinth, Paul said, should greet and show love to the unknown Titus who was being sent by another church (2 Corinthians 8:23–24). Similarly, when Paul visited Judea, the believers there celebrated his life story even though they had never met him prior to his arrival (Galatians 1:21–24).

There is other evidence of church-to-church support as well. Paul and Timothy, for example, were known to celebrate the strengths of other churches (2 Thessalonians 1:4). And some groups of believers financed Paul's journeys so that he would be able to serve churches outside of themselves (2 Corinthians 11:8).

Not to focus on the negative, Church, but we disillusioned are not always sure we've adequately maintained this sense of connectedness in our current-day congregations.

Our lack of connectedness is perhaps well illustrated by a 2003 Duke Divinity School report entitled "Experiences of Protestant Ministers Who Left Local Church Ministry." In it Dean R. Hoge and Jacqueline E. Wenge identified the most common motivations pastors cited for departing full-time ministry. Three of the top six reasons were rooted in internal church conflict: conflict or lack of support within the denomination, conflicts with church members, and doctrinal conflicts.[2]

Doesn't exactly scream connectedness, does it?

Along these same lines, I have observed how rarely I hear of churches or denominations *merging* with each other. Yet I can't count the number of times I've heard a horror story about a church or denominational split. The World Christian Database says it all when it denotes not one, but 9,000 Christian denominations.[3]

The Mobility Line

Another line that sometimes seems invisible today is the one that shows the mobility of the early church's mission. First-century believers seemed to have an unusual draw toward taking their mission on the road. At times, perhaps, they had no choice in the matter. At least once, the church was forcibly scattered (Acts 8:1). But even so, they did not cease in their activities. Rather, they used their new locations as opportunity to make their message portable (11:19).

Even when the church wasn't forcibly scattered, the leadership often willingly dispersed. The early church was notorious for sending people out from their groups: Barnabas to Antioch (Acts 11:22), Barnabas and Paul and their crew to Phoenicia and Samaria (15:3), Judas and Silas to Antioch, Syria, and Cilicia

(15:22); first Timothy and then Titus to Corinth (1 Corinthians 4:17; 2 Corinthians 8:18). Paul, the original church-letter-writer, always seemed to be in circulation. He and the mobile Silas were said to travel around "strengthening churches" (Acts 15:40–41).

The church's ability to take on a "portable" nature also seems consistent with the experience of Old Testament gatherings of God-followers. When the people of Israel had a permanent place of gathering, the temple, God's presence dawned in a special way (1 Kings 8:10–11). Yet, before this point, God's presence also fell on his people minus any formal place of meeting. As they traveled together through the wilderness, for example, God appeared via cloud in the day and fire at night (Exodus 13:21–22). And let's not forget that a movable tented structure at one time housed God's presence along the Israelites' journey (33:7–11).

While the disillusioned appreciate the churches that have invested in artistic facilities, high-tech sound systems, coffee bars, and cafes to make their meeting spaces more attractive, we reflect that the early church's mission seemed to be less focused on remodeling the home base and more to do with getting outside of it.

Maybe the focus on portable spirituality is what draws a disproportionate number of twentysomethings to Theater Church in Washington, D.C., where pastor Mike Batterson estimates almost 80 percent of its congregation are twentysomethings. Furthermore, he notes that 50 percent of this young crowd were de-churched (meaning they had left the church for a period of time after previously attending) and 25 percent were unchurched (meaning they never attended church previously).

Why does this church attract so many twentysomethings, you might wonder. For starters, Mike thinks Theater Church's marketplace location—the Regal movie theater on the fourth floor at Ballston Common Mall—appeals to twentysomethings who he says are "a little gun-shy about institutional church."

I myself was attracted to find out what Theater was all about after spotting the phrase "Wear Your Faith" on one of Mike's websites. When I asked him about it, he explained that half of Theater's congregation are "Hill staffers" who shape the political policy of our nation. Tuning into these young people's desire to be "difference-makers," Mike and the crew at Theater began tweaking the church's agenda to equip attenders to be and live church in the context where they spent the most time. To help them integrate their faith into the 166 hours or so a week they weren't in church, Mike and his church adopted a rule of thumb: "If it doesn't help someone live out their faith Monday to Friday, it's not worth saying."

George Lings, director of research for the Church Army, seems to be thinking along similar lines. Lings has challenged Christians in his arena to admit that some encounter Jesus more effectively outside the church. Calling the church, among other things, a sometimes "invisible relic of the past," Lings kicked off the church planting seminar at the twentieth Christian Resources Exhibition, the largest event of its kind in Europe, by insisting that more should be done to demonstrate the range of what contemporary church is.[4]

House church zealots like Wolfgang Simpson, who wrote *Houses That Change the World*, also seem to be prodding the church in an outward direction. "It is time to change the system," Simpson says. "Luther did reform the content of the gospel, but left the outer forms of church remarkably untouched. The Free-Church freed the system from the state, the Baptists baptized it, the Quakers dry-cleaned it, the Salvation Army put it into a uniform, the Pentecostals anointed it, and the Charismatics renewed it. But until today nobody has changed the superstructure. It is about time to do just that."[5]

Perhaps the best way to underline Simpson's point is to note the increasing attraction of house churches. After online web resource House Church Central had been live only twenty-one months, its searchable directory had registered over two hundred house churches and attracted an average of forty-two queries per day.[6] Another site, *www.housechurch.org*, lists thirty-one churches in my home state, among a long list of other home-based churches that meet in the United States, Canada, and almost every other country you could think of.[7]

Among other non-building-based expressions of church are a number of online sites that twentysomethings frequent to experience spiritual interaction.* A few of these include The Ooze (*www.theooze.com*), Dtour (*www.dtour.com.au*), Gink World (*www.ginkworld.net*), Ship of Fools (*www.ship-of-fools.com*), ReJesus (*www.rejesus.co.uk*), MethodX (*www.methodx.net*), Next-Wave (*www.next-wave.org*), Off the Map (*www.off-the-map.org*), Thunderstruck (*www.thunderstruck.org*), and maybe the most popular, *Relevant* magazine (*www.relevantmagazine.com*).

Relevant magazine strikes success with twentysomethings for an oh-so-obvious reason: the guy running the show is a twentysomething himself. Cameron Strang, twenty-nine at the time I write this, created an edgy online site about faith and culture that might make some Christians uncomfortable. In fact, its first print issue was banned from the bookstore at Strang's college alma mater, Oral Roberts University.

When it comes to Strang's efforts with the Relevant website and their corresponding line of books, not everyone is calling for a ban. Phyllis Tickle of *Publishers Weekly* calls Cameron a leader in what she terms the "new Protestantism." "These kids [the minds behind Relevant] just excite me to death. They are the first wave of what Christianity is going to be like in a post-denominational age," Tickle told *USA Today*.[8]

One could argue that all of the aforementioned examples, from home-based ministries to websites, qualify as "church" or "assembly" according to New Testament descriptions. They all involve gatherings of God-followers (albeit, sometimes virtual ones). And because of this, we can affirm that God very likely

---

*According to the Pew Project, 64 percent of Americans have used the Internet for spiritual or religious purposes. Check out *www.pewinternet.org/PPF/r/126/report_display.asp* for more information.

works in all of them. After all, wherever two or three are gathered in Jesus' name, he is in the midst of them (Matthew 18:20).

Unfortunately, from house churches to websites, even our dreams of the more-perfect church do not escape disillusionment's incredible wingspan.

Sadly, just about any activity or faith affiliation—old or new (even websites!)—can quickly become "institutional" if we allow it a disproportionate amount of spiritual space. Along these lines, the emergent church, popularized by Brian McLaren, is often criticized for having institutionalized some less-than-stellar ideas.

For the record, McLaren is one of the more compelling church leaders I've heard and even on the occasion when I don't swallow every sentence that comes out of his mouth, I have appreciated the questions he brings to the forefront of the Christian world. Despite the fact that he has always insisted emergent is just "a conversation" and not a movement to convert to, he and his peers have still drawn criticism from people like D. A. Carson, author of *Becoming Conversant with the Emerging Church.*

Carson's warning to the emerging church contains some heavy words: "If emerging church leaders wish to become a long-term prophetic voice that produces enduring fruit and that does not drift off toward progressive sectarianism and even, in the worst instances, outright heresy, they must listen at least as carefully to criticisms of their movement as they transparently want others to listen to them."[9]

Outright heresy? See, even when you don't mean to start a movement, sometimes other people start forming one with your ideas. And, even worse, some people start acting like your movement is *the movement*: the one that has the answers for every church under the sun. And that attracts critics who worry your movement could excessively or unwisely influence the larger Christian world.

It's no wonder the disillusioned can't help feeling that a little despair lines our church clouds. Why do all of these gatherings eventually succumb to some kind of institutional dysfunction? What is the unfortunate common denominator that seems to eventually discolor each of our attempts to bring church to expression? The weakest link seems to be the people.

Sighhhhhhhh.

Thanks to the imperfect nature of its participants, every kind of local church we imagine or bring to expression is marked by human flaws, missed expectations, and disillusionment. It seems you will always struggle to raise hope higher than your own dysfunctions, Church. This perhaps is the most disillusioning realization of all.

As a result, some twentysomethings are no longer convinced that a person's dysfunction, disunity, or other ills would be eliminated if we could just get them to sit in a church building on Sunday morning. Ditto on the world. If we could cram every human on the globe into every available pew or cushioned theater seat, we don't think they would necessarily become infused with hope or increased desire for connectedness.

Instead, we cling to the hope that we will arrive at increasingly accurate definitions of *church* as we continue to seek God's intentions. Similarly, when we draw pictures of the church for our children, we want those images to look less like a steepled building and more like the latitude and longitude lines embracing every inch of the globe. Any given coordinate on these lines, we hope to tell our kids, marks the presence of groups of people God has brought together to live out his values in any number of ways that may or may not be housed in a building.

Discussion Questions

1. Do you find that your experience of church is consistent with the church described in the New Testament? Why or why not? In what ways is it consistent? In what ways is it not?

2. Who drew the first lines that defined church in your life? What were the lines?

3. Do you question any of the lines that found their way into your definition of church? If so, which ones?
4. Do you agree or disagree with the lines (Attendance, Success, etc.) the author questions?
5. What lines were present in the New Testament church that are perhaps underemphasized or absent in today's church? The author named two. Are there others that strike you?
6. Does today's church have to borrow from the New Testament model? What traits do you think are most important to maintain from biblical times? Which ones can be sacrificed?
7. How can today's church encourage people to search out God's ideas for themselves, rather than just relying on church programs to enhance their spiritual growth?
8. Do you believe that websites or house churches could qualify as church? Explain your answer.

Key Observation

When offended by the practices of a particular group of Christians, it is wise to suspend judgment toward all religious institutions until we have examined whether these practices are consistent with biblical ideas about church.

Don't Want to Be the Church Anymore

Dear Church,

I know you're all about living up to Jesus' expectations for you, but sometimes the word *church* just doesn't have that ring to it. Know what I mean?

Like I kinda want to whisper the word sometimes. Not because I'm ashamed, because well, I know better than to be ashamed. Don't think I'm not aware of that verse.* I can recite it in my best monotone-KJV-memorizing-Scripture voice, if you want.

I want to whisper the word *church* because I know that as soon as it leaves my mouth, someone in the room will flinch, inevitably thinking of steeples and crosses and roadway signs sporting interchangeable cheesy sayings. It's like playing one of those psychological games where I say the word and everyone else says the first thing that comes to their minds. Only when I say "church," they tell me their reactions with their eyes, with their body language, and yes, sometimes with their mouths. And let's just say, the "gee, tell me more" reactions are hard to come by.

I want to whisper the word *church* because sometimes the person in the room who is flinching is me. Because, despite all the amazing, mind-blowing images that come with any institution appointed by Christ himself, the term *church* has developed some negative connotations even for me. So sometimes I resort to saying it softly, or kind of half-mumbling, half-coughing it out

* See Romans 1:16.

into conversation without pausing to let someone point out that they can't understand my slurring.

Sometimes I just skirt mentioning the C word altogether. Not to sell my faith short, you understand, but to get around all the assumptions attached to the label. Unfortunately, it is not easy to describe your brand of Christian faith without affiliating yourself with an institutional church.

Simply saying that I'm a Christian would be an immediate giveaway, of course. Christians go to church. Churches are full of Christians. Everyone sees the connection.

I can't really go around telling people I am "a person of the Way" because that brings to mind cults and stories of churches gone bad, like David Koresh and Jim Jones. And there are enough people already who think the local Christian churches are cults as is. Heck, it's our favorite churchy joke to recount how the neighbors heard that people in our "cult" light candles at late-night services and get what they're sure is garden-variety Crisco oil slapped onto their forehead at various prayer meetings.

I can't say I'm "an evangelical," because that is even worse than being a church-going Christian. Evangelicals are those people who preach a rotating list of twelve sermons all written to describe the eternal torment of hell. They are the people who play eerie music as the pastor asks people to raise their hands or "come forward." Or if they are on TV, maybe they ask you to touch the screen where the static electric charge doubles as the spark of the Holy Spirit.

I can't say I'm "a conservative," because then it beckons images of men with three-piece suits and neatly parted, shiny hair who build coalitions to defeat the Democrats, the Smurfs, and billions of other alleged tools of Satan.

I can't say I'm "religious," because we've all been taught the folly of that. Now everyone say it together: "This is not a religion, it's a relationship."

I can't say I'm "a Jesus Freak," because although I do know D.C. Talk's rap by heart, I like people to wait in suspense a while before deciding I'm a freak. I don't want to tell them right from the beginning. It takes the fun out of it.

I can't say I'm "spiritual," because people translate that as a simple "two thumbs up" for Mel Gibson's *Passion* movie. Or they figure I subscribe to an online horoscope and watch TV shows about channeling my dead pets. Spirituality is very in, you know. My waitress, dry cleaner, dentist, and grocery store cashier all have WWJD bracelets and copies of *The Prayer of Jabez* to prove it.

The emergent church opts for "Christ-follower" which, I have to admit, is the best term I've got as well. (But darn it, I don't want to be pigeonholed as "emergent" either.)

I wish I could land on a self-description that's new and fresh, something not so stained in people's minds. The only problem being, of course, that eventually too many Christ-followers (myself included) will show their humanness and our *new* words will be blacklisted from the usable list too.

Maybe instead of worrying about labels, Church, I should be taking the advice of Francis of Assisi: "Preach the gospel at all times. If necessary, use words."

Maybe I should demonstrate that "going to church" infers something broader than keeping a pew warm in a cross-clad building. Maybe it's time to rewrite the age-old, folded hands illustration: *Here is the church. Here is the steeple. Open the door and see all the people.*

Here's my edited version: Here is the building; it doesn't need a steeple. Inside is the church ... see, the church *is* the people.

Perhaps I should make it clear that church, at its most basic level, is just a big group of Christians. And then I could point out that *Christian* was never supposed to be a synonym for "perfect," "blameless," or "never hypocritical." We already have a synonym for that. It's *Christ*. The two words sound similar, and look similar on paper—and obviously there's an inescapable relationship between them—so it's understandable that people sometimes get confused. But, thank God for us, they are far from identical twins. Mistaking even the best Christian for Christ is like seeing your first Model T and walking away thinking you've met Henry Ford.

Maybe we should revamp the newcomer's orientation. You know, touch on the disillusionment piece. Maybe we should tell potential converts about our various shortcomings upfront.

(Note: We used to call potential converts "seekers," but apparently the cool term is now "inquirer." Although I think "inquirer" sounds like someone who buys up those checkout lane magazines about Elvis's three-headed dragon living in a box of Cheerios. By the way, when it came to vocabulary, Jesus cut right to the chase. He called the unsaved "lost," and he said it in a way that made the lost sound like the treasure we should all be out looking for. Now that's cool.)

Regardless of the lingo, maybe we should let potential Christians know that no one in the church keeps all the standards spelled out in the manual all the time. Unfortunately, to my own discredit, I slide here and there, sacrifice a few rules when I'm in a hurry or if it's convenient. Maybe I should tell them that I strive to perform at my maximum capacity ... well, except for when I'm tired, or cranky, or acting in my own self-interest.

Maybe I should point out right from the beginning that there is a reason why Jesus is the head honcho and I am the company gofer. That no matter how many promotions I get, he's actually the only one who is following procedure all the time. We try to keep up, but we can't. And the really annoying part? He's not even following guidelines. He just is that way naturally.

Maybe I should try to help newcomers separate God from me. Hey, a good start on that lesson would be to stop acting like I *am* God. Stop acting like I know exactly what to say, what to do, how to think, how to live every moment of every day. Stop projecting that I am the ever-so-useful-and-always-accurate judge, jury, and executioner all in one.

Maybe I have to realize that if I want disillusionment to change, the first person who has to change is me.

Discussion Questions

1. Can you identify with the author's upfront admission of embarrassment about the church? If so, explain.
2. Did you find it hard to hear the author's criticisms of the faith? Why do you think that is?
3. What parts of the author's commentary, if any, were offensive to you?
4. Do you feel the need to defend the church whenever it is attacked?
5. Have you been prepared to offer textbook explanations when people express doubt? Do you think this helps? Why or why not?
6. Does your church, or other local churches you've attended, ever discuss people's skepticisms or criticisms of the church? Why or why not?
7. What terms do people in your church or community use to describe followers of Christ? Think both positively and negatively.
8. What term do you prefer to describe followers of Christ? Which word or label, if any, do you identify with most?

Key Observation

Any new religious practice or movement—
if given disproportionate spiritual space—can
quickly become institutionalized. Therefore, rather
than focus on changing the church, it may be
wiser to focus on changing ourselves.

part 3
Introducing Hope

Sick of Being Disillusioned

Dear Church,

I wasn't convinced you'd still be reading at this point.

Not that I think you're short on stamina, but some of these letters are less than flattering. If I toss out one criticism too many, I worry they might "accidentally" get incinerated during a reckless night of campfires, s'mores, and Kumbayah.

Don't worry though. My everlasting chain of criticisms is about to come to a halt. I just can't keep up this pace much longer.

Frankly, I'm getting sick of my own disillusionment.

The fact that I can't breathe or blink or just "be" without feeling jaded makes life seem like a scary Ferris wheel ride. I feel like I'm trapped in a car stuck halfway up with no chance to move forward or to get out and see the world from a different perspective.

I never liked Ferris wheels much anyway.

Hence, I've decided that I need to find a way to end this disillusionment spree, if for no other reason than the fact that my cynicism isn't righting the world any faster than my ideals.

There's got to be a way to move past my issues with the church. And there's got to be a way for my generation, and perhaps some others, to move on too.

Of course, when I suggest my generation may be able to "move on," some of my peers start to get suspicious. They worry that after voicing my generation's disillusionment publicly, I will cave to institutional pressure. That I will make it sound like twentysomethings and other disillusioned groups can just "get over it" and plug back into the church by sundown.

I understand their concern.

Overcoming disillusionment is just not that simple. It's not a twenty-four-hour flu bug that disappears after a day of rest and fluids.

Unfortunately, it is much more chronic than that.

Disillusionment has all the signs of a serious illness. It tends to persist over a long, indefinite period of time. It often involves multiple recurrences. And it can be virtually invisible to people who meet you, so much so that people in your local church might not even realize you're infected.

When I say that the disillusioned and I may need to move on, I'm not saying that our disappointments are invalid or that we should minimize our concerns. I *am* saying that we should take disillusionment for what it's worth, but also understand that its merit has an expiration date.

On the plus side, our disillusionment with the church can cue us into things that just aren't right. It can alert us to actions that don't align with God's intentions or behaviors that aren't even congruent with our own stated objectives.

Disillusionment can serve a prompting role in our lives. It can fast-forward the growth of our convictions. Give us the extra push and courage to stand up and say, "This is not how church should be. This is not what God wants people to experience in his community."

In other words, stages of disappointment with the church are most valuable when they inspire us to get off our religiously-bogged-down booties and actually do something to help better represent God's purposes to our world.

But my own disillusionment usually loses its positive value somewhere along the way. Sure, I may start out rightly grieving my disappointments with the church. And this stage of grieving might even legitimately last a long time. But when it gets to the point where I'm spending more of my life being disgruntled than I spend living in hope, I think it's safe to say I've lost track of my center.

After all, it makes sense that disillusionment might discolor the way we see the world for a while. It does not make sense, however, to let disillusionment permanently take over our lives—to let it dictate how we see the world, how we make choices, or how much hope we feel in the day to day.

When despair starts to gain totalitarian control of our ability to live out our Christian mission—turning us into pathological cynics who would rather swallow live tarantulas than speak a positive word about organized Christianity—it is *probably* a sign we have entered into unhealthiness. Probably.

And disillusionment does more than just steal our favorite pair of rose-colored glasses. Ongoing disenchantment with the church can lead to spiritual fatigue and worse, a breakdown of one of the most essential components of our relationship with God: our ability to have some faith.

Not to mention, if disillusionment causes us to leave our local churches, it may also separate us from another Christian life force: the larger community of believers.

It gets even scarier.

Sometimes I get so caught up in being disappointed with how the church falls short of God's ideals, that disillusionment almost *becomes my god.*

That sounds ridiculous, I know, but unfortunately it's true.

When disillusionment begins to monopolize my head time or prevents me from seeing or acting in hope, it consumes too much of my energy. The sheer minutes I spend journaling my negativism, complaining with my peers, or even relentlessly complaining to God start to take away from the minutes I could spend living toward solutions to my concerns.

When I let my dissatisfaction with church direct how I respond to people or events, it's like turning the day over to disillusionment. And every time I allow myself to be influenced by these same disappointments, I give disillusionment another day. Before long, I've pledged weeks, months, even years to discontentment. I begin, in effect, to give my life—not to Jesus—but to disillusionment.

This kind of unexpected idolatry—the obsession with living in despair over what is wrong with institutionalized church—creeps up on you (like most shifty little idols do). No one ever asks you to repeat a prayer and ask disillusionment into your life. No one ever asks you to read a membership manual explaining your ongoing commitment to disillusionment. Just the same, criticism becomes what we end up worshiping.

There is some good news in all of this, though.

If disillusionment becomes a false god, it is not an all-powerful one. It does not hold us prisoner. It does not own us, give us life, or make us all we are.

Rather, in many ways, we own disillusionment. We own disillusionment because we, together with our fellow world citizens, manufacture it.

After all, our disappointments are generally a result of mankind's collective sinful nature, a result of living in a cursed world where we no longer have rows of free fruit trees, garden strolls with God, and eight hours a day to spend naming our pets.

Instead of this fantastic, whimsical garden, we have all these flawed human beings who only have a rough idea of what is going on, trying to live out the intentions of the perfect and all-knowing Creator.

We're all a little like the crazy person who stands on the city corner and proclaims himself to be *the* prophet who God chose to declare the exact day the world will end.

As Super Prophet stands there shifty-eyed and unshaven, dressed in military fatigues, and weighed down by a backpack full of his belongings, he hollers "God's message" at the very top of his lungs. Interspersed with God's message are other "lesser" messages—for example, conspiracy theories that suggest God is communicating when the world will end through fortune cookies at the local Chinese buffet.

As you can imagine, people don't pass by Super Prophet saying, "Wow, check out God's messenger."

Um, no.

Everybody who walks by is thinking, *Look buddy, you're a nice basket case and all, but if you're the prophet God chose to deliver us, I think I'll take my chances trying to slide by without your religion.*

Super Prophet's flaws are easy to see because he is wearing them outside his skin. Anybody within a yardstick of his position can smell that the guy hasn't had any recent encounters with a bar of Ivory and can see the remnants of his breakfast Egg McMuffin on his shirtfront. They notice how jittery he is as he paces around; they hear the paranoia in his voice; they notice the logical fallacies in his presentation.

But what is harder to see is that everybody in the church is at least a little like Super Prophet.

It's especially difficult to notice because many of us are phenomenal actors. Working without a script, we ad-lib our way through the Sunday morning church routine with Oscar-worthy performances.

We know how to work a sanctuary. How to walk down the red—or sometimes tacky, multicolored Berber—carpet shaking hands, kissing babies, and giving people quick squeezes. We know to flash a winning smile and how to project just the right tone of voice when we offer hellos and how are yous. We know to call people by their first name and to try to make personal comments that make them feel important.

We are schmoozing machines.

But you know what? Despite our professional Christianity, despite our wealth of brownie points within the volunteer pool in our local congregation, we are way too much like Super Prophet than we want to admit.

There are days when we don't want to bother to dress up and please the crowd, days when we spout things that don't make sense, even days when we probably want to stand out on a street corner and scream curses at people.

And even though we may not own the official Super Prophet fatigues or backpack, our soul's internal sense of style is often an equally repulsive fashion disaster.

We may have amazing aims, impeccable motives, and incredible determination. But we still do the things we don't want to do. We're still blind to our own flaws. Even the best of our intentions often end up hurting people.

Maybe we shouldn't believe that we are God's messengers either!

Or *maybe*, we should leave some room in our heads for the idea that the church — which is made up of a bunch of messed-up, flawed people who sometimes just happen to take a shower and shave — isn't going to be perfect either.

I don't know why this is such a revelation. We expect flaws from other groups of people, like used car salesmen, politicians, or celebrities, but when it comes to the church, we're complete suckers. Or at least I am.

I don't know why I think anyone with the ability to match their clothes, read the Bible, and teach without stuttering also must have a pure thought life and be impervious to temptation. I don't know why I think anyone with a great singing voice, a standard acoustic guitar, and a little rock and roll in them must have an amazing devotional life and a carefree marriage. I don't know why I think people who have mastered the art of passing out bulletins have risen above anger management classes, gossip, and parenting problems. And, most of all, I don't know why I think that just because people all lump together and buy their own building in the name of Christ, that they will always — without fail — act like true representatives of Christ.

Could I get any more unrealistic?

Sometimes, I wonder how my experience with church would change if I could just make a few mental adjustments. What wound happen, for example, if I honestly admitted that I am likely to encounter one or more of the following church flaws?

- People may not always appreciate the hours I've invested volunteering.
- People may not always take the time to understand where I'm coming from.
- People may not always care about some of the things I value most.
- People may not always offer the kind of support I need when I need it.
- People may sometimes pressure me to live up to their expectations.
- People may turn my mistakes into material for gossip.
- People may act in a way that seems "fake."
- People may get caught up with the wrong priorities.
- People in leadership may do things in their personal lives that make me admire them less.
- People in leadership may sometimes make bad decisions that end up hurting the church.
- People may seem to ignore certain portions of Scripture.

Is it possible that just by changing some of my expectations, I could influence my own ability to contentedly engage Christian community? If I simply realized that every church or group of people—no matter how exciting or brilliant—is infested with all kinds of flaws, would I respond to their failures differently? Would I draw different conclusions?

Instead of seeing apparent failures as a contradiction of all the church stands for, instead of seeing them as reason to throw out institutionalized church as a whole, instead of seeing them as evidence that the ideals of God himself might somehow be tainted, what if I just thought: *Whoops. There's another flaw. Stupid curse. Thankfully, God is in this with us, because this one is going to sting.*

Along these lines, I've decided that maybe the church should introduce a type of "premarital counseling" for people considering commitment.

Here's how I imagine it would work.

You walk into a room. There, sitting behind an official-looking desk, is an especially wise counselor wearing a very serious pair of glasses, pen and clipboard in hand.

You feel a little uneasy.

Wise Counselor introduces himself and then gets right into the session. "So, tell me why you think you want to commit to this congregation?"

You freeze. You know there are absolutely tons of things you love about this congregation, but you're worried you won't be able to convey the true breadth of your adoration in a couple of concise, convincing statements.

"Well, I really appreciate the emphasis on the Word of God," you say, hoping that calling the Bible the "Word of God" will get you a few extra points.

Wise Counselor doesn't say much. Just an "uh-huh" as he checks something on the paper in front of him.

Apparently he wants you to say more.

"And I really enjoy the people. The community, I mean fellowship, is so important to me." You chide yourself for almost forgetting to use the word *fellowship*.

Wise Counselor nods. You go on.

"Not to mention I love the worship. The song leader is very talented. She really knows how to invite the congregation into the presence of God."

You allow yourself a quick smile, feeling like you've touched on all the religious bases.

Wise Counselor raises a suspicious eyebrow in your direction. He sets aside the clipboard with the evaluation that you may have just failed and stares at you. He seems to be purposely trying to increase the amount of awkward tension in the room.

Just when you think Wise Counselor's eyes have bored a hole into your inner thought chamber and you are about to confess that as a toddler you colored on Jesus' face in your children's Bible storybook, he finally cuts the silence.

And then you wish he wouldn't have said anything at all.

Wise Counselor leans forward. "Now tell me some of your church's flaws."

"Um..." You stall while analyzing all your possible responses. If you say you think your church has no flaws, you will certainly seem like you're caught up in blind love. But if you say it has too many, it might seem like your love is insincere.

"Well, sometimes the Sunday morning coffee runs out before everyone has a cup."

This seems like a safe place to start.

You can tell Wise Counselor is not impressed.

"And, um, I've noticed that on certain weeks, there are some particularly obvious typos on the media screen."

He's tapping his fingers and gazing into space. *Boring.*

"Not to mention that sometimes there is a really loud microphone thud or a lot of feedback over the speakers. You hear this high-pitched squeal and then you see the service producer calling back on the telephone to tell the sound guys to get their act together."

Now you're getting to the good stuff.

But Wise Counselor is tough to win over.

He stares at you a moment longer, as if summoning the right amount of anger to deliver his next lines.

"But what if one day the sermons get boring? Let's say, perchance, they don't seem to relate to you."

You gulp.

"Let's say your fellow attenders don't seem to care about you at all! Let's say they just seem to be using you to get you to serve those horrible fifth graders that no one wants to teach in next year's vacation Bible school?"

You try to hold still, but you know you are visibly squirming in your chair.

"Let's say one day, the worship leader goes tone deaf. What would happen if she suddenly couldn't sing on key, or worse yet, if she started singing every single verse of every hymn in slow motion?"

You wonder if you're supposed to respond, but pray the questions are rhetorical.

"What if the pastor fails you?

"What if the nursery leader runs off with the head usher?

"What if the church uses your tithe to buy thousands of burger flipper souvenirs for their upcoming message series 'Serving It Up God's Way'?

"What if it gets to the point that you can't invite your pastor and your worship leader, your board members, or your Sunday school teachers to the same Christmas party because of how much they distrust and dislike each other?"

Your mind is spinning in a million directions.

"Do you love your church enough to stick with them through all of that? Do you love them enough to love them even when the emotions run low and the feelings of excitement have worn off?"

Wise Counselor's voice is increasingly louder. The lights above his desk seem especially hot.

"Are you in this for better or for worse, for richer or for poorer, in sickness and in health?" As he spits out these last words, Wise Counselor's fist slams down on the desk, creating a small earthquake that disrupts all the papers.

Slowly, out of the corner of your eye, you begin looking for the nearest emergency exit.

Then, just as suddenly as it rose, Wise Counselor's voice softens.

"I'm not trying to scare you away or anything," he drawls in a mild-mannered tone.

You manage to nod even though you wish you could curl up in the fetal position.

Wise Counselor continues, "But you can't let anyone tell you that committing to a church is all fantasies and fairy-tale endings. You can't think that once you become a member that things are going to magically fall into place, that every day is going to be one more day of happily ever after.

"Committing to a church isn't easy. It takes a lot of hard work. You're not perfect. Your church isn't perfect. A lot of imperfect things are going to happen along the way. Sure, you're going to have your exhilarating highs, but you're going to have some rock-bottom lows too.

"You're going to encounter some flaws in the church that you never knew about or suspected. You're going to see that the church doesn't really value all the things they claim to value. Someday, you're going to start to feel like the church is a totally different organization than it was before you committed to membership. You're going to wake up one day and wonder what possessed you to join the place."

Wise Counselor smiles. "Once the honeymoon stage ends, then what do you do?"

You don't even try to answer this one.

Thankfully, Wise Counselor likes to hear himself talk.

"You might think about leaving the church. But if you do, just remember, every church has its own set of flaws. Sure, you might find another church that seems attractive, that seems to excel in the areas where your church falters, but beware! If you join another church, you won't find the perfect church, you'll just find a completely different set of flaws.

"Scared? Good!"

You're noticing Wise Counselor has a flair for the dramatic.

"But, thankfully, you know who to run to when you're scared. Ultimately, you see, your commitment is not to this one local church. In fact, your commitment is not even to the global ideal, the church at large. Your commitment is to God.

"And as long as you nurture your relationship to God, and you draw closer to him, you will also find the ability to sustain your relationship with your local church."

And then, with one statement—"We're going to give you a couple weeks to think this over"—Wise Counselor's spiel is over. He hands over a waiver to sign so your church can prove that someone has explained the potential risks involved in joining their congregation if you decide to do so.

What do you think, Church? Are you logging onto *monster.com* to post an ad for a Wise Counselor position on your staff?

Okay, okay. Maybe the approach to preparing people for real-life church doesn't have to be quite this extreme. But don't miss what I'm saying.

We need to understand that neither the local congregation nor the collective of all the believers on the planet is perfect.

If we expect it to be perfect, we might as well lie down and whistle for disillusionment's steamroller.

But let's not talk about disillusionment anymore for now. Like I said, I'm sick of it. If I never hear the D word again, it will be too soon.

Discussion Questions

1. Have you ever been disillusioned so long that you grew sick of your own disillusionment? Explain.
2. Why do you think the author's generation is skeptical of "quick-fix" solutions to some of the church's problems?
3. Do you think that it is important that every stage of disillusionment eventually ends?
4. Have you ever been so disillusioned that your critical thoughts started to control the way you looked at the world? If so, share how this unfolded for you.
5. What, if any, unrealistic expectations have you placed on the church?
6. What expectations might you need to change in order to see the church in a truer light?

7. How is your commitment to the church similar or different than a marriage commitment?

8. What part of Wise Counselor's comments sticks with you most?

Key Observations

When disillusionment begins to monopolize our head time, preventing us from seeing and acting with Christ's hope, it detracts from our mission and can become, in itself, a type of false god.

If we expect that churches — communities of flawed humans — will sometimes fail, we may be less likely to become disillusioned when they do. After all, human failure does not equate to failure of God or his ideals.

Progress Isn't Painless

Dear Church,

I know. I know.

I haven't always taken Wise Counselor's advice.

Call me a fair-weather friend. A bandwagon Christian. A wishy-washy believer. I have attempted — more than once — to abandon you, Church. However, as it turns out, I am not particularly successful at running away.

I think I get my talent in this department from my mother. She once told me a story about when she tried to run away as a child. She packed her bags and set off walking. Unfortunately, she wasn't allowed to cross the street without a grown-up, so she had to return home.

Likewise, it seems I've been born into a generation of church runaways — some of whom never got too far from home. I suppose you could liken us to kids who got mad at our parents, packed up our knapsacks, and took off to the tree fort in the backyard.

As we're camping out on the outskirts of the church, many of us are still involved in the church's story. We engage in daily dialogues about faith both in person and via the Web. We invest our time in meaningful activities (like community service) that reflect our alignment with Christ's mission. We still live in rich community with our Christian friends who we allow to speak authentically into our lives.

Although we may not necessarily be in church every week, many of us still consider ourselves unofficial extensions of the church's mission.

We kind of want to be affiliated with the church, but we kind of don't.

This letter, then, is written to the attention of those who are conflicted about their relationship with the church. It is for the indecisive people who may have run away from our local congregations only to pitch our tents on the church lawn.

As we try to decide whether to continue to invest in the institutional church, here is my humble suggestion. Before we pack our U-Hauls, forward our mail, and relocate to some distant philosophical peninsula far away from the church, I think we should pause to acknowledge one timeless truth that applies both inside and outside the church. And that is this: *We shouldn't expect progress to be painless.*

As far as I can tell, great things usually come at a price.

Life bears out this principle time and time again.

Take birth pains for instance. I've yet to attempt childbearing myself, but I've watched enough women gritting their teeth while hissing "hee-heee-hooooo" on the big screen to know if my house ever catches fire, the first thing I'm saving on my way out the door is my birth control.

Beautiful newborn babies, it seems, emerge via physical and emotional struggle.

College is often the same way.

You can't get on to learning the fun stuff until you sit through the painfully tedious prereqs—all of which are conveniently available in three-hour-long night classes. (And somehow, a course in ancient Greek mythology is absolutely necessary to success in any career field.)

I have slowly come to believe that pain is a necessary part of the process because it provides the incentive to adopt needed change or growth.

Rarely, for instance, do churches roll out change while what they're doing is working smoothly. Not that the committee members drafting the local church's next five-year plan aren't wild and edgy in their own way. But let's face it, they usually aren't the type to strap the church onto the local fairground's Tilt-a-Whirl and give it a spin just for the rush. Sometimes they need a little pain to push them along.

Minus the pain, church leaders can seem to have this unwritten cardinal rule that we kind of tack on to the end of the Romans Road when no one is looking. *All have sinned and fallen short of the glory of God ... The wages of sin is death, but the gift of God is eternal life through Jesus Christ our Lord ... AND ... If it ain't broke, don't change it.*

Or as some almost-translations say: If it ain't shattered into millions of unrecognizable pieces *and* on fire, don't change it.

So yes, the sanctuary wall may be cracked, but puttying the cracks would be a painfully tedious process. Not to mention, it would change the way the wall has looked for the last twenty-five years. Admittedly, services may be occasionally interrupted by avalanches of crumbling plaster, but that's nothing a few "Beware of Rock Slide" signs affixed to the ceiling fans can't resolve.

Then one day, an entire beam wrenches itself loose and flattens four deacons and a worship team member. Suddenly, pain reawakens the leadership's common sense. *Well, maybe we could take a look at that wall ...*

And so they have to temporarily suspend their happy thoughts and venture out of Never Never Change Land in order to purchase at least a *small* container of plaster.

Granted, the wall scenario is a humorously exaggerated example. But if you've had your eyes open, you've probably begun to suspect that the church is not *really* exempt from the effects of the curse. Sometimes we only get to enjoy progress and ongoing peace after we undergo inconvenient and sometimes painful periods of change.

Unfortunately, if you're anything like me, no one ever gave you a handbook that spelled out how pain might play out in a church context.

Somewhere in my first year of college, I realized that adult life doesn't always go exactly the way we want it to. As a freshman, I had applied to be a peer advisor for the following year. And yes, a peer advisor sounds like something anyone can do by just dispensing some casual advice to a peer. But this particular position, called a P.A., was different because *they paid you*. And in college, money is the sixth love language.

So I interviewed. Tried to convince the hiring panel that if they gave me the job, students would camp out for days and line up around the dorm for miles to hear my guru-on-the-mountaintop-caliber advice.

But you know, the panel was worried about how the lines would block traffic … so they didn't hire me.

There I was, a college student who already had a number of burdens—all of which seemed especially paralyzing at the time, but just happen to be slipping my mind right now. (Who wants to bet they had something to do with those particularly troubling creatures called boys?) And Student Development just hauls off and doesn't hire me.

The *nerve* of some people, huh?

And so, I quickly entered all my circumstances into my handy-dandy, little Christian calculator, which immediately spit out the equation: disappointment = college must not be in God's will.

Unfortunately, my dad was surprisingly resistant to my well-conceived plan to immediately quit college and fly off to some remote village—which I would choose by closing my eyes and pointing at a globe—to do missions work of any kind. *At least the natives will appreciate my leadership!*

I remember being somewhat skeptical as Dad sat across from me at the world's slowest fast-food restaurant and told me that periods of difficulty or pain are not completely accurate indicators that God wants you to abandon your current commitments overnight.

I was not sold on Dad's theory right away, but being there's that one verse about having a long life if you respect your parents, I decided to listen through at least *one* ear.

Then my dad brought up Psalm 23, Church.

And I was thinking, *Tell me he didn't just say Psalm 23 — the infamous Shepherd's Psalm! Does he know how many cottonball sheep these hands have made?*

But when your dad is my dad (i.e., someone who can turn a peanut butter and jelly sandwich into an altar call), there is always some wild card you never really counted on.

And my dad says, "You know Psalm 23, right?"

Do I know Psalm 23? Puleeeze ... did Noah's kids have chores?

Just for good measure, I began rattling it off in the most bored tone I could muster. "The Lord is my shepherd, I shall not want.... He maketh me to lie down in green pastures ..." (Um yeah ... all PKs who are worth their salt know the KJV.)

My dad nodded, satisfied that my third-grade memory verses had stuck. "So where are you when his rod and staff are comforting you?"

Ahhhh, weren't you listening? (I quickly repeat Psalm 23 to myself.) "In the valley of the shadow of death?"

"And where is the table where your cup runs over?"

"Um ... (repeating it again) ... in the presence of my enemies?"

Thus ended another course in What They Never Taught You in Sunday School. Apparently, those "hard times" parts of the faith had been there the whole time. The Bible-makers just subliminally blended that stuff into the memory verses to trick us into not realizing it wasn't there. (Well, that's one theory anyway.)

And, apparently, my dad was not the only one in on the conspiracy theory.

My friend Ron Martoia, a pastor I would later work for, said some things that were suspiciously similar. He said that the older I got, the less I would have the luxury of seeing things in these black-and-white categories where everything matched up exactly as I thought it should.

Bill Hybels, founding pastor of Willow Creek Community Church, must be in on the secret too. I once heard Hybels acknowledge that staying faithful to the church was sometimes so difficult, all a person could do was "put one foot in front of the other."

In fact, the more I investigate, the more I'm convinced that people have known about the flaws of the faith for *centuries!*

Take Saint John of the Cross, who lived five hundred years before me. John wanted to bring changes to the Carmelite order of monks. But when he voiced his criticisms of the church, they locked him away in a prison cell.

(Did I say *I* had some criticisms, Church? Because really, I don't feel that they are criticisms as much as they are points of discussion. So, um, no need to go to all that trouble of turning down the bed in the prison cell for me. I'm cool. Thanks.)

While imprisoned, Saint John of the Cross wrote a series of reflections entitled *Dark Night of the Soul,* which describes how periods of pain are integrated into our "normal" rhythms of life.

John points out that during painful moments, God is still giving good things, but because life has lost its "felt" sweetness, our eyes filter out the good and we remain in a state of seeming emptiness.

John goes on to note that pain may be a valid part of God's plan, a useful element of Christian experience. Because God is no longer revealing himself through the highs of ordinary human experience, we must struggle with God and our painful circumstances. And in this sometimes intense reflection, God often reveals things in the darkness that we would never stop to examine in the light.

Maybe this is the same process Paul was talking about in Romans 5:3–5 (NIV) when he said, "We also rejoice in our sufferings, because we know that suffering produces perseverance; perseverance, character; and character, hope. And hope does not disappoint us, because God has poured out his love into our hearts by the Holy Spirit, whom he has given us."

How's that for mind-boggling? If Paul is right (and, of course, the inspired nature of the Scripture seems to suggest he is), then suffering is actually linked to the production of hope.

In my disillusionment, I often saw suffering or pain as reason to abandon hope. However, I seem to be wearing the verse inside out. It's through perseverance and character-building that suffering actually produces even greater hope!

In light of this, Church, I've slowly grown to suspect that the dark moments define the Christian faith, and its church, just as much *or more* than the bright ones.

If this is true, then Bill Hybels' definition of faithfulness, "putting one foot in front of the other," seems like one of the most realistic ones. And I'm glad Hybels said it this way too. I have a feeling that my generation needs such grounded, nonairbrushed definitions of faith.

For us, when it comes to the church, we may sometimes feel like running away. More than once. And we may even run away. More than once. But for us, faithfulness may be resolving that somehow, someway we will keep coming back.

Discussion Questions

1. The author describes herself and some of her generation as runaways to the tree fort in the church's backyard. Have you ever run away to such a ridiculously close place? Explain.

2. Why do you think we expect progress to happen without pain?

3. Have you ever really thought about the apparent pain evidenced in the Shepherd's Psalm? Why do you think we tend to focus on the good parts of this passage rather than the tough ones?

4. What other Scriptures or lessons from church tradition suggest that progress is not painless?

5. Think through the words of Romans 5:3–5. Has suffering in your life ever produced hope? Share what this experience was like.

Key Observation

When we expect progress to be painless and easy,
we set ourselves up for disappointment. It is often
when we push through the darkness that we see
opportunities to grow and improve we
never would have seen in the light.

The Best Dirt
I've Ever Eaten

Dear Church,

In my previous letter, I mentioned that my definition of "faithful" is not as idealistic as it used to be.

When I was younger, I imagined that being "faithful" would entail some sort of heroic deed—preferably one that would warrant regular standing ovations.

I envisioned one of those five-smooth-stones acts of faithfulness where I would awe the audience by flooring a Philistine giant with a miraculously well-aimed curveball.

The faithfulness I've inherited, however, seems a bit less flashy.

My variety doesn't seem to involve parting the Red Sea or striding across the surface of the Sea of Galilee. And, much to my own disappointment, I don't seem to have been assigned any secret weapons. No high-powered slingshot. No powerful staff to wave around. No jar of oil that never runs dry. (Heck, some days I'd settle for one of those conveniently packed bat belts à la Batman and Robin.)

On the contrary, sometimes the best faithfulness I can muster is really not very faithful at all.

My faithfulness is often much less like single-handedly defeating my country's most fearsome enemy and much more like, um, let's say *running away*. And, as we know, this method typically warrants a much less glamorous reception, such as an all-expense-paid vacation in the stomach of an enormous fish.

I imagine, though, that the real value of being trapped in a fish's belly is the opportunity to realize how you have contributed to your devolution to a human appetizer.

Sure, day one you may be dreaming up plans to cruelly torture all those annoying little Ninevites for their inability to do what God wanted. It's their disobedience that led to your stay in the belly of the fish to begin with, right?

But by the time day two rolls around and you've been ingesting fish fumes for a full twenty-four hours, you likely begin to make some important distinctions. Like, *well, maybe I shouldn't stir-fry* all *the Ninevites. Maybe I'll just skewer their leaders. After all, they're the ones who are really calling the shots.*

By day three, when you start to realize that your existence is now equivalent to a ninety-nine-cent bottle of fish food at your local superstore, I bet perspective *really* sets in.

After it's no longer dodgeball-esque to juke the other food particles the fish keeps swallowing, I'd guess you get to a point where you hate seafood so much you vow to burn down every single Long John Silver's on the planet.

You probably start to think that you are the worst scum to ever walk the face of the earth. No, no, no ... you're the *bacteria* on the scum ...

And suddenly, your pride is no longer impairing your view to see things God's way. In fact, you have a complete change of heart. You're willing to be best friends with all those chummy little Ninevites. You'd crawl back to them on your hands and knees, begging to polish their little Ninevite shoes for them if only God would forgive you.

Wait, what is that rumbling sound?

Suddenly, you find yourself facedown in a pile of sand that — in comparison to your previous surroundings — is the best sand you've ever tasted in your life.

Believe it or not, lately I can relate to Jonah quite a bit. I often feel as though I am lying facedown on the shore with a mouthful of sand.

I feel this way because, for a while, I was convinced that *someone*, *somewhere* owed *me* an apology (or at the very least, an explanation) for how the church had failed me. As a result of my logic, my emotions were full of bitterness: I felt used, I felt abandoned, I felt misled.

One day, in a moment of dark reflection, a friend asked me, "Why do you feel like you need someone to give you an explanation for your disappointments?"

I staggered backward.

Why *did* I need an explanation? Why *was* I letting my own peace depend on other people's willingness to express regret for the pain I had experienced?

As I tried to answer this question, other questions arose. Wasn't I — a member of the global church, not to mention a former staff member in a local church setting — just as responsible as any other party for how the church failed its members? Why didn't *I* ever feel the need to apologize on behalf of the church to those who had been hurt?

When you think about it, I guess that most people never get an apology for the way the church hurts them. Sure, we all do our part in contributing to the church's shared mistakes, but when it comes time to take the blame, we seem to lose our individuality. All of the sudden, the church is just one faceless, nameless, ownerless institution that can't own up to its failures.

I decided this was not okay.

It wasn't okay for me, for my generation, or for anyone else to experience pain at the hand of the church and then have the church just keep on plodding forward as if nothing had ever happened. Somewhere along the line, I thought, someone should legitimize and apologize for the wounds of the injured.

I wondered how the church could help release people from this type of pain. The kind of confusing pain you feel when it seems like God himself, through his church, has rejected or insulted you. I wondered whether any one of us could help dissolve some of the burdens church people carry by looking them square in the eye and admitting that the church has not always been what it was supposed to be.

The more I thought about the idea, the more real it became to me. I found myself wanting to help resolve the sorrow attached to so many people's interactions with the church. I wanted to tell as many people as I could, face-to-face, "This pain and rejection is not what God intended for you to experience in Christian community. Please forgive us for the times when we have failed to act like the community of Jesus-followers we claim to be."

As "out there" as this idea seemed at one level, I had a strong motivation to see it executed. So I decided to put forth a strange request. I asked the elders of my local church—ironically, a church I had tried to leave and returned to more than once—if I could offer an apology. I told them I wanted to ask forgiveness not only for some of the hurt I may have inflicted on others, but for some of the hurt that people may have experienced at the hand of the church at large.

Because of a very unique set of circumstances, this church, which happened to be undergoing some reevaluation, found the spirit of the idea appropriate for an upcoming meeting.

I soon found myself sitting on the stage and saying, "Some of you are long overdue for an apology." I proceeded then to bawl through a lengthy series of apologies, intertwined with jokes about how mascara (which now was running down my face) was the world's worst invention.

When I finished, my reception was overwhelming. Dozens of people made the effort to find me before they left that evening. Grabbing me by the sleeve, I was told, time and time again, "Thank you *soooo* much. That was so important for me to hear. You have no idea how that released me from some of the pain and bitterness I had been experiencing."

Honestly, by that point, I barely cared about their benefits. I was experiencing the climax of my own freedom from burden and bitterness—quite possibly, the freest moment in my entire Christian experience.

I was dumbfounded before God that just one moment of simultaneously given-and-received grace had somehow healed a thousand previous pains.

Somehow, for that moment, I couldn't feel disillusionment's sting anymore.

I emerged from that night thinking that even just a few minutes of experiencing such intense, shared grace was so sweet that I would never want to live my life without it again. And I resolved that in the future, I would be much better at noticing opportunities to offer apologies and to usher in what little piece of God's grace I might give to others.

That said, I can't help thinking that this might be one of those times, Church. A chance to acknowledge the hurt swirling around beneath the surface of the larger Christian community. And a chance to express my regret that the church at large has sometimes hurt people on a historical and international scale.

And so, people of the church, I want to offer an apology to you on behalf of the institution you belong to.

To lead pastors and missionaries, I am sorry for the times when our spotlight has left you sunburned. We've often encouraged you to perform as though you are always on stage, waiting for the affirmation of our applause. But there are times where you too should be allowed to be privately human, to make mistakes that people don't print in the bulletin or pass through the prayer chain. I am profoundly sorry for the times we have squeezed you under the world's largest microscope and tediously examined all your flaws.

Pastors, I am sorry for the times we have made you the church referee, forced to make split-second decisions knowing that, no matter what you choose, half the gym will criticize the call. I am sorry that you have lost sleep and tears and maybe a little blood, bearing the weight of heavy decisions. That we've sometimes squashed you between a rock and a hard place, and when you finally chiseled your way out, we criticized your methodology.

Our 20/20 hindsight makes the "right" call seem so ridiculously simple that we've often been outraged that you missed it.

I am sorry that our behaviors might have forced you into some unhealthy habits that took a toll on your own emotional well-being and that of your family. I know that sometimes you had to develop calluses—thick skin that could sustain you through the times when no one seemed to support you. And I'm sorry that those calluses sometimes spread to your heart, so that you couldn't feel or connect with your congregation any longer. I am sorry that we may have forced you to be hardheaded, to charge ahead in warrior-style leadership, because it seemed impossible to get a consensus from your perpetually divided people.

And, perhaps more than anything, I regret the times when we have affirmed you in ways that substituted you in the place of our Savior. For the times we have been carelessly willing to follow you in any direction and put our hopes and faith in your intelligence or leadership above even the God you serve.

I am sorry that this misplaced allegiance to you, rather than Christ, may have brought out the worst in you. That it may have launched an addiction in some of you, encouraging you to chase after the admiration of others before the blessing of God. I am sorry for a wide range of destructive behaviors this may have caused: perfectionism, depression, willingness to exploit others, fear of failure, oversensitivity, guilt, restlessness. I am sorry that we sometimes tied accountability to whether the church was "bigger" or "flashier" instead of whether it was "deeper" or "holier."

I am so sorry, pastors, that you can do a million things right and still be nailed to the ground for the one thing you do wrong. And I'm sorry that too few people have had the guts to voice their concerns to your face rather than to their small groups. I am especially sorry for the guilt and rejection that you have been unable to separate yourself from when people criticize your local church or the church at large. You have taken responsibility on more than one occasion for problems you never contributed to.

I read the following quote from Teddy Roosevelt and it reminds me of my admiration for you pastors who continue year after year.

> It is not the critic who counts, not the man who points out how the strong man stumbled, or where the doer of deeds could have done them better. The credit belongs to the man who is actually in the arena; whose face is marred by dust and sweat and blood; who strives valiantly; who errs and comes up short again and again; who knows the great enthusiasms, the great devotions, and spends himself in a worthy cause; who, at best, knows in the end the triumph of high achievement; and who, at the worst, if he fails, at least fails while daring greatly, so that his place shall never be with those cold and timid souls who know neither victory nor defeat.[1]

Lastly, I am sorry for the loss you experienced when friends and team members walked away from your shared mission. Despite your obligation to bless their departures, it couldn't have been easy to watch these companions exit the journey. I am sorry for the disappointments you felt in your soul when yet another person discarded the church context that you could not as easily abandon. Thank you so much for staying the course.

To the families of pastors and missionaries, whose identity within their local church family is often so tightly tied to their spouse's or parent's post, I humbly apologize. I am sorry for the times when your individuality got swallowed up by titles like "missionary kid" or "pastor's wife." I am sorry for the times when this loss of personhood stripped you of your own right to grow and think and forge new ministries of your own. I am sorry that people saw you for whose son you were or whose wife you were rather than for who *you* are.

I am sorry that you sometimes gave up your husband or father to lead the "world" into wholeness, but no one seemed to notice when you or your family was hurting. I am sorry that we sometimes thought Christmas cookies and greeting cards could sustain you through all twelve months of the year. I am sorry that we failed to realize that your family is human as well, that there were pain and hurt in the everyday, and therefore a much more consistent need for encouragement and gratitude. I am sorry if we fostered an environment that didn't allow you to talk about when you were hurting or in trouble.

I am sorry for the unrealistic expectations that we sometimes anchored to your lifestyles. That we thought you should somehow be able to grow up or grow old without making the mistakes so many of the rest of us are permitted to make. That we pressured you to be the example, when sometimes you're the one who needed the extra support and maybe—just once or twice—we could have strived to be a role model for you.

Kids, I am sorry for the times we have attacked your parents, not realizing that you *were* old enough to know exactly what was going on. Not understanding that you felt each blow we delivered to your dad or mom. Not comprehending how we stripped the church of its warmth for you, how our actions made God's institution look like a monster who was thirsty for your parents' blood. I am sorry that our own carelessness, immaturity, or desire to be right took away the comfort and familiarity that had once made the local church feel like your second home.

Most of all, I am sorry, kids, for the times you saw the local church deliver so much destruction that you lost your desire to be part of the church at all. I'm sorry for the times your gifts got short-circuited, for the moments when you went from wanting to be on a church staff yourself to wanting to avoid the church at all costs.

And on that note, I pray that you won't let our failures prevent you from exercising all the ideas and talent God put inside you. God's inspiration in your life is not what fell short. It was us. Go and grow up and with our heartfelt blessing lead the best local churches this world has ever seen. We believe in you.

To the elders of local churches, I am sorry that you have borne the criticism of people like me—who have never had to face the decisions you face or bear the responsibility you bore. I am sorry for the long hours and late-night calls that enlarged your personal burden with churchwide issues of both enormous magnitude and minute detail. I am sorry that in your faithfulness, you have had to be the remnant crew who manned the church even when it seemed like a ship that would surely go down in the storm. And that you often did it without people caring how much responsibility you shouldered ... or even knowing who the elders were ... that is, until you made a decision they didn't like.

Please surrender your feelings of hurt, blame, and inadequacy and know that even in the times when you failed, you failed while attempting the noblest of causes. And let us give you, at least momentarily, our honor. Regardless of the outcome, rest easy knowing that whenever you tried to serve us from pure motives, you served us well.

We are truly indebted to you, elders. And if we were smarter, we would thank you so much more often.

To church staff, I am sorry that there is no time clock to destroy the misconception that you work only one day a week. I wish that everyone in the church could log onto a website and see live-camera footage of you working ridiculous amounts of overtime, filling in when others bailed, or coming early to open up and staying late to close. I sometimes wish your phone records were accessible to the public so people could readily see how many hours you spend counseling and troubleshooting to enhance their discipleship.

I am sorry for the times when people became angry at you because you couldn't stretch yourself far enough, couldn't meet their every demand, couldn't be available every time they needed a resource or a word of encouragement. I am sorry that you were our "fix-it people," the ones we went to when *we* needed something and that it all too rarely crossed our minds that you might have needed something along the way as well. I am sorry that you have had to live in a state of confusion—wondering at times whether you accomplished more good than you did bad. You did, by the way.

Really. You'll never understand how much good you did.

I am sorry for the times our commitment to you has failed to rival our commitment to our kids' bake sales or our home redecoration. That we have casually strolled by, noticed a problem that we could help address, but then speed-walked in the other direction. I am sorry for the times that we have made you beg, go to vision casting seminars, and read leadership books to manipulate us into doing what we should have been doing out of the natural motivation of our heart: helping serve. I am sorry that we sometimes looked for the least we could do instead of the most we could do. I am sorry that we called the church "*our* church" but that when it came to hard work, we sometimes translated this to mean "your" work.

I am sorry we never realized that when we called at the last minute to say we couldn't fulfill our ministry obligation, we were only one of several backing out ten minutes prior to service start. I am sorry that, as a result, you may have spent the first half hour or maybe the entire service running around panicked, trying to do multiple jobs at once to make sure our church's adults, teenagers, and children were served. I'm sorry that because of our failure to follow through on our commitments, you sometimes never got to sit down and go to church yourself ... or that when you did, it was far less enjoyable because you had to constantly worry about how some area was short-staffed.

I am sorry if our consumeristic expectations challenged you to become more efficient and more successful workaholics. If we made your job description so many miles long, or piled so many hats onto your head, that you were forced to live in a state of constant frustration knowing that you could do nothing with excellence. I am sorry for the times when we acted as if we were the only people you needed to please when, in reality, implementing our personal suggestions meant earning the disfavor of some other group in the church that held the opposite opinion. I am sorry that we sometimes backed you into a corner and then ridiculed you for sitting there.

I am sorry that we always forgot to send you that note of encouragement or to call and praise you for a job well done. And even more sorry that we remembered somehow to call and let you have it when things didn't go the way we wanted.

To all of you who serve in this capacity, I pray God's fullness upon your lives. Though many times we Christians casually offer the promise "I'll pray for you," when it comes to you, I sincerely mean it. May God bless you and your families for your day-to-day faithfulness.

To volunteer leaders, I am sorry for the times you came to the staff looking for clarity or support but walked away empty-handed. For the times the church staff have not been able to rise above their own challenges to source you, love you, invest in you, and maintain intimacy with you like they intended.

I am sorry for the times when we church staff have acted like you should have no life outside of our ministry areas, that you should be available any day of the week any time of day to assist with routine and emergency operations. I am sorry for the times we staffers became overdependent on those of you who could be counted on to do what you said you would do, how we pushed you to serve in too many services, for too many months in a row, without giving you an often needed reprieve.

I am sorry for the times the staff expected you to put the rest of your life on hold, but then failed to repay you by taking your suggestions and advice seriously. I am deeply sorry if we treated you like you or your ideas didn't matter when you were—in many ways—the very backbone of our institution.

I am sorry if we taught you to draw affirmation and motivation from the wrong place. If we spent more time training you to expand our attendance or increase our recognition than we spent encouraging you to truly, truly know God.

Let me just say what you have perhaps not heard often enough from the pulpit. And that is this: God cares far more—and I mean *far* more—about the condition of our souls and the genuineness of our relationship to him than he will ever care about our ability to keep all our services and ministries spinning flawlessly.

So if we have made you feel like you had to earn our favor, let me now encourage you to take the time to breathe deeply and really get to know our Jesus intimately. This is what is really important. Despite all our other encouragements, if you know one thing, know this: The moments when your heart is well ordered before our God are the moments when we are *most* proud of you.

To church attenders, I am sorry for the weekends when you were overlooked. When no one said hi or remembered your name, when no one invited you to their small group or included you in their postservice plans. I am sorry for the times when no one noticed you were absent or hurting … or both.

I am sorry for the times when we offered you more programs than friendship, more books than honest dialogue, more encouragement to be like us than to be like God. I am sorry for the times we asked you to serve in our ministries, to fill open service slots, without offering you the dignity of true friendship with us and our teams.

I am sorry for the times we sent messages that would conflict with the example of Christ when he walked this earth. For the times we looked down our noses, scowled, or flashed cold stares in your direction. For the times we acted like we "on the inside" were somehow better than you "on the outside" and made you feel as if, by struggling uphill, you might someday be "good enough" to make our inner circles … to be one of "us."

I am sorry for the times we pushed you too hard and asked you to take steps that you were not ready to take, to carry burdens you were not ready to bear. And, on the other hand, I'm sorry for the times we let you keep our seats warm, but never prodded you to shed your anonymity and join in the game. I'm sorry for the times we tried to be your heroes, to hide our flaws from you, instead of just letting you help us and love us and understand us for who we are.

I am endlessly sorry for the times when our failures have misrepresented God, made you doubt the Bible, or jaded you toward the church at large. Please know that it was us, and not Jesus, who failed you. And if you never set your foot in a church again, please know that it is God who hears you in the stillness and distance of where you are and who will trump our narrow minds in welcoming you into the kingdom if you align yourself with him.

Forgive us for the times we failed to be the Christian community God wanted you to experience. You deserved better.

To those outside the church, I am sorry for the times we underassessed your intelligence by assuming a few "cool" service elements, rather than real relationships, would draw you into our churches.

I am sorry for the times we presented Christianity as a three-step plan that you read and signed as if it were some type of credit application. That we sometimes acted as though Christianity and Christ were so simple and tidy that we could neatly package them inside a little box that you should be able to open and transplant into your spirit without any questions or hesitation. I am sorry that we sometimes brokered fire insurance — get-out-of-hell-free cards — instead of inviting you into God's fullness. I'm sorry that we sometimes forgot to exemplify "kingdom" in this world ... never mind the next.

I am sorry if we approached you or didn't approach you based on external criteria like your socioeconomic class, skin color, education level, or any other trait that made you more or less like us. I am sorry for the times our message has isolated you, made you feel more judged than forgiven, or offended your family, friends, or people group in a way that was not biblical.

I am sorry for the times that we acted like your mistakes were worse than our own. I am sorry that we failed to realize that life is hard, just generally hard no matter who you are, and that we weren't generous enough with grace and compassion unless it worked to our benefit.

I am sorry that we locked our doors when we drove through your neighborhoods or shirked you when you tried to talk to us in the checkout lines. That we spent more time avoiding you than really getting to know you, that we wrote you off before we even knew your names or stories. That we pretended to understand where you came from, when really we had never bothered to truly listen.

I am sorry when we acted like faith and doubt could never coexist, like it was wrong for you to have questions about why God allowed evil in the world, instead of encouraging you to ask the questions and grow through them. I am sorry when we acted like there were answers to every question when there are some questions we just can't be sure about, that only God knows the answers to.

I am sorry that we sometimes told you what to believe, and how to believe, instead of letting you really discover and own your journey for yourselves.

I am sorry that we sometimes cared more about whether you came to our church or our choir concert or our youth group or our Bible school than we cared about whether you knew how to live in God's fullness.

After all you may have been through, I understand if you have given up on the people within local churches, but please don't give up on our God. In the times we have made him out to be less than he was, cheapened his church by shaping it via our agenda instead of his, we have committed terrible offenses. Forgive us or don't, but know that in our smartest and most sensible moments we would forget our pride or our desire to be the "most spiritual" and we would get down on our knees and beg you to reconsider the Savior who is eternally more noble and just than we are.

You must know that even if you can never respect the church, even if you doubt everything that comes out of our mouths, the one thing that is still true is that Christ wants relationship with you and that opening yourself up to him would be hands-down the best investment you could ever make in your life.

And if you do come to follow Christ, I pray that you follow better and more closely than the rest of us have.

Most of all, I am sorry we haven't apologized more often or sooner.

To the church at large, I am sorry for the times we saw one Christian or group of Christians fail and assumed the worst of all Christians. I am sorry that we often put you in the place of Christ, expecting you to be blameless and mistake-free when that was never the identity you were supposed to bear.

I am sorry that we have failed to appreciate your role in bonding society; in providing not just six weeks of visits to a professional counselor, but a lifetime of community with real people. I am sorry that we didn't always understand how you contributed to society's well-being both nationally and internationally. I am sorry that we have mocked you in our comedy sketches, political cartoons, talk shows, and disillusionment-heavy books.

I am sorry we didn't always honor you like a *Bride* magazine cover girl on the moment she swings open the sanctuary doors to walk down the aisle on life's brightest occasion. We would do well to remember, Church, that this is who you are to our Lord.

We are eternally glad that you exist for the generations before us, for us, and for our children to come. And lastly, don't worry, Church, there are still those of us who will protect you until the last breath.

And to Jesus our head, I am so sorry for the times when we heard your clear direction, but postponed our obedience to siphon just a little of your glory for ourselves. I am sorry for not trusting that you alone — if lifted up — draw all people unto yourself more than any plan or strategy that we could contrive. I am sorry that we sometimes tried to operate as a ghostly institution floating around with no head, acting separately from you and by our own power.

I truly regret the times we reduced "faith" to regimented formulas for success. And I'm embarrassed that when our human thinking failed to produce the kind of supernatural results we were looking for, we somehow still blamed you for the deficits. I am sorry for how we have sometimes abused your freedom and crafted a version of you to suit our own purposes.

I am most sorry for the times when the way I lived as "church" didn't project what you intended, when the Jesus I described flew in the face of your actual persona, when the God I worshiped wasn't really you at all ... but reflections of you (like success or perfection). I am sorry for not realizing the satisfaction to be had in being teamed in your mission. I am sorry for wasting a day, a breath, a dollar, for acting like "I had given my life" when I was actually keeping it for myself.

I know it must seem like I am constantly distracted, that my priorities are misaligned, and that I allow way too many causes to compete for the life that was supposed to be yours. But know, that in the moments when I am most sane, when I am most clear on who I want to be, I want nothing more than to know you.

And know that I want to be more sane and more clear in more moments, so that tomorrow I will know you and love you even more than I know you and love you today.

You know, of course, that I am not even wise enough to know all the things that we should be sorry for, Jesus. So forgive me, and forgive all of us who call ourselves church, for the times we have both knowingly and unknowingly sinned and for the times we will inevitably err in the future. And thank you for your ongoing patience and investment in helping us grow at our pace and according to our own capacity.

In closing, thank you, Church, for being willing to listen as I try to respond to a humbling lesson in my own life. And know that I am resolved to do better in the future than I have in the past. If I am aware of unaddressed hurt, I want to do more than just simply wait around claiming someone owes *me* an apology. I can suck it up and be the first to eat dirt. And you know what? If this is landing facedown in the sand, I have to tell you, I am with Jonah. This is the best sand I've ever tasted in my life.

Discussion Questions

1. Have you ever felt like someone somewhere owed you an apology for something that happened in the church? If so, explain.
2. Did you have a hard time moving forward without an apology or explanation? If so, why do you think that was?
3. Have you ever felt partially responsible when you saw someone become jaded with the church? If so, what did you do? Was there anything you could have said or did say that might have brought some measure of justice to their experience?
4. Which of the author's apologies, if any, hit you the hardest? Explain your answer.
5. As you read the author's apologies, were you convicted about something you may have done to hinder the well-being of someone else in your church? What could you do to right any possible wrongs?
6. Think of a time someone has shown you undeserved mercy. How did it affect your relationship with them, your ability to serve in the church, or your outlook on life?

Key Observation

It is easy to focus on how others in the church could apologize to us, rather than owning our own role and failures as we live church to the world around us.

P.S. Following are some things I've learned about forgiveness. If there is someone in your life who you need to forgive, rather than reading these "lessons" all at once, I suggest you turn back here each day and reflect on one at a time.

Fifty Things I've Learned about Forgiveness

1. Learn to apologize even if it seems risky or unnecessary; it is usually neither.
2. Apologizing for what you have done wrong does not mean that the person you are apologizing to bears no guilt. It just means you forgive them whether they ever understand or regret what they've done or not.
3. If you can't apologize, it is sometimes just as beneficial to simply acknowledge someone's pain.
4. Don't ever deny someone the luxury of being human or broken. That is not a luxury you yourself can afford to lose.
5. Don't ever forget that given-and-received grace is the very premise of our salvation. Without it, none of us would be whole enough to forgive anyone in the first place.
6. On a secular pop-psychology level, you have a "right" to a lot of anger and hard-core bitterness. But then again, what does pop psychology *really* know compared to God?
7. When you tell people they need to repent, they often don't understand the real benefit of restoring themselves to you. Before you air their mistakes, make sure that they understand how deeply you value their relationship and how desperately you want to maintain it. People most often respond with humility when

someone casts a vision that offers them the benefits of true grace.

8. Don't relentlessly demand an apology from people who cannot see the error of their ways. Instead, trust that God's Spirit can travel into the inner recesses of their hearts where you yourself cannot go.

9. Don't purposefully numb yourself to those who have hurt you to protect yourself from further relational tension or loss. Putting up walls never creates more connectedness and detaching yourself never repairs the distance between you and others.

10. Realize that total restoration may not come all at once. If it is to come sincerely, it may need to unfold in stages. Be patient.

11. Do *what you can* to pursue unity *as you can*. If you wait until tomorrow, things may have spiraled too far out of control to ever take back.

12. Only God knows the motives of a person's heart. Don't pretend you do.

13. Always value humans most. Saving a relationship with a person is much more important than adding another accomplishment to your resumé.

14. Live generously. Make routine "deposits" in the lives of those you are teamed with so that if you ever have to make a "withdrawal," you will have something to withdraw.

15. Don't store up your frustration. You will be tempted to let it out when it is not appropriate or helpful to do so.

16. Speaking poorly of someone is like training yourself to think the worst of them. Soon you will find that they are monsters—not because they have no actual strengths, but because you have conditioned yourself not to see them.

17. Speak the truth in the small things. It will make engaging the big things so much easier.

18. Don't ever write off a relationship as too far gone. Our God is a God who helps us transcend the impossible.

19. Don't tie your ability to move on to any particular pace or outcome. Rather, commit to investing in restoration over the long haul.

20. Any time you get the chance, speak words of restoration and grace, and encourage others to speak them too. In doing so, you create a culture that reflects Christ well.

21. Do what you need to do even when the other person isn't planning on doing their part. You wouldn't want to sacrifice your ability to live in God's blessing just to spite them, would you?

22. Avoid secret grudges, manipulative conversations, or wishy-washy go-betweening. Do everything you can whenever you can to live openhearted before all parties involved.

23. Acknowledge your own failures in trying to bring about restoration. Admit when your approach has been or is imperfect, and communicate that you are trying and want to try even harder.

24. Guard your emotions, especially when you are in leadership. People who follow you in the light will often also follow you into the darkness. Do not be responsible for taking them there.

25. Tell people what you have learned about how you could have conducted yourself better in the past. By sharing your own failings, you encourage others that it is safe for them to acknowledge their flaws as well.

26. Realize that often far more is at stake than whether you are deemed right in the end or whether the other party ever speaks the exact confession you've written out for them in your head. Other people learn what forgiveness is by how you act. Thus, the kingdom will be well served if you err on the side of generous, rather than stingy, expressions of forgiveness.

27. Do what you know is right so that you can live with a clean conscience. Do not reserve your apology for the moment when the other party is also ready to apologize. Why should you take bitterness to the grave just because they never choose to be humble?

28. Love those you are teamed with more than you love your own pride. If you don't, then what you are offering is not really love at all.

29. How long should you wait for the other party to desire restoration? As long as it takes. If you truly love them, you will live your whole life ready to usher in greater unity at a moment's notice ... no matter how long that moment takes to arrive.

30. Stick by your do-the-will-of-our-Father family just as fiercely as you stick by your genetic family. Which do you think is stronger: our spiritual bond or our human one?

31. You will rarely find stronger love than the kind that results when someone knows your flaws, and vice versa, but you choose to love each other anyway.

32. If forgiveness or restoration is not instantly achievable, then let it be known that you will be there in the mess and you will be there when the mess resolves—all the while hoping that one day things will get better.

33. Don't be quick to disassociate from others because of their flaws, or their inability to acknowledge them. Our God is not quick to disassociate from us.

34. Realize that our own flaws and pain often impair our ability to see. Our lack of objectivity often makes others' motives seem far more calculated than actually is the case.

35. Because of our own bias, other people's mistakes are often far more obvious—and seemingly far more amplified—than our own. Know that your mistakes look the same way to them.

36. Don't say you have done everything you possibly can to achieve unity if you have never actually addressed a problem directly to someone's face.

37. Get everyone at a table and talk things out before everyone has time to become cemented in their individual status as victims.

38. Remember Jesus told the disciples that those who acted in his name could not easily deny him the next moment. Start by feeling unified in God's mission, and work your way up from there.

39. Remember that offering forgiveness is as much an act of furthering the kingdom as any other task on your to-do list.

40. Even if you do not speak your grudge, it is what is inside your cup that makes you unclean. Don't kid yourself by telling other people you don't have a grudge. It leaks out of you when you are not even aware you are dripping.

41. If whoever wants to be first must be last, it makes sense to sometimes be willing to go to the end of the line.

42. If you are only willing to forgive when people do exactly *what* you think they should do *when* you think they should do it, then what you are offering is not grace at all, but rather yet another chance for others to applaud you for being the one who was right all along.

43. The way we go about being right is as important as being right. Sometimes the way we go about being right destroys the value of being right.

44. Don't split the church over your own personal preference. Do you really think God will think the loss to the kingdom was well worth what you sacrificed trying to be right?

45. Remember that when you fail to live in unity with those who are in God's church, your children will take note of your decision. How do you want your children to remember you?

46. Sometimes in our anger we miss opportunities to express love and support when people have failed and need that love and support the most. We would be well served to backtrack and offer the grace that we forgot to give on so many occasions.

47. Often the best way to progress in the future is to make peace with your past so it cannot travel with you to tomorrow.

48. The reality behind truth claimed to be spoken in love is that it was often not spoken in love at all.

49. When we keep a record of people's wrongs, we're more likely to look for their wrongs in the future.

50. At the end of your life, you will never wish you had read one more book or completed one more task from your inbox. But you will certainly wish that you had one more day to love someone more deeply.

An Idea from a Guy Named Jesus

Dear Church,

Hey there! How are you doing today? Great weather we're having, don't you think? And how about those Tigers?

Okay, okay, you're right. I have no idea how the Tigers are doing this season.

I'm stalling. And not doing a good job at it.

I confess, I've been purposely avoiding a certain topic ... a certain question. A question that has come up almost every time I discuss these letters.

Inevitably, when I tell people that I am trying to write about disillusionment with the institutional church, they ask, "How is your writing going to end? You're not going to encourage people to leave the church, are you?"

Hmmmm. Am I going to encourage people to leave the church?

That is one incredibly loaded question.

When you ask it, do you mean will I encourage people to leave their *local congregations*? Or do you mean will I encourage them to abandon Christ's ideal for Christian community?

If you're questioning whether I'll insist that my peers get their names back on the local church's weekend worship roster, then I'll have to get back to you on that in some future letter. But if you're wondering if I'm going to try to shoot holes through Christ's vision for his followers, then you can set your worries aside.

Are you kidding me? I *am* the church—or at least part of it. If I stabbed the church like that, my own flesh would bleed.

Besides, do you remember what kind of faith systems dominated this planet before the church?

Think back to the beginning with me. Life started out wonderfully, but went downhill from there.

God had manufactured a place, Eden, that was the perfect context for community. In this garden incubator, where the spiritual and the physical worlds merged, humans came into contact with God's very presence. He actually walked among them and spoke to them face-to-face.

Can you imagine how intimately humans could have understood God and his ideals if we had picked them up in a sensory, multilayered, hands-on classroom like Eden?

But, of course, we never got to learn all of Eden's lessons thanks to Adam and Eve, who exchanged God's ideal for a new dish from Satan's recipe book. No different than their modern-day counterparts, Adam and Eve's attempt to control God's ideal—to get what *they* thought they should get of Eden—got them kicked out of God's intended experience. And really, as a species, we've been kicked out of God's intended experience ever since.

Starting with the moment Adam and Eve traded garden walks with God for a free sample in the produce section, every attempt at spirituality has been tragically marred with disillusionment.

Let's start with some of the BC years' finest organized religions.

Where were the ziggurat* gods when the Babelites started speaking ten different dialects of mumbo jumbo? Where were Egypt's gods when blood came pouring out of their faucets? Where was the Philistines' god when their colossal warrior was struck down by a scrawny shepherd boy? Where was Nebuchadnezzar's god when starved lions failed to eat their human

*Ziggurats were layered buildings that often had a temple to some sort of god at the base. Some posit that early peoples believed the gods dwelled in the mountains and would thus prefer mountainlike towers like the ziggurats.

appetizer? No doubt the Egyptians, Philistines, and Babylonians knew their share of disillusionment with religion.

But it wasn't just these alternative religions that came up short of God's intentions for human community.

Even the Israelites, God's chosen community, allowed their spirituality to devolve into a genetic tagline. Rather than solely embrace the Edenlike Promised Land God was directing them toward, the Israelites crafted their own ways to get what they wanted when they wanted it.

For instance, remember when the Israelites escaped Egypt through a retractable path down the middle of the Red Sea only to later get impatient with God's pace and begin praying to the apparently-amazingly-powerful statue of a cow (which they had carved only moments beforehand)?

I don't know about you, but when the little cow-statue just stood there and looked back at the Israelites with its beady little cow-statue eyes, while standing on its four little motionless cow-statue feet, I'm guessing that some disillusionment was going on. *It appears our religious system may contain some sort of flaw.*

But, of course, this was not the Israelites' lone attempt at manipulating their religion to serve their own desires or timeline. Remember when they stacked their military's loss column by erecting altars to Baal rather than trusting in the real God who would have protected them from foreign enemies? Again, at this point, as their armies were being wiped out at record-breaking speeds, I'm thinking someone somewhere in Israel was disillusioned. *Man, I have a feeling I could have just eaten all that lamb I sacrificed to Baal.*

So goes the Israelites' flawed attempts at being the community of followers God intended them to be.

They spat in the faces of prophets, forgot temple purity laws when it worked to their convenience, married the gods of the nations they wed into, and demanded a political system headed by a hopelessly human king. A king who more often than not got his royal backside and the entire nation into more than a cubit of trouble, mind you.

Hence, faulty attempts to create the perfect society scarred the world from Creation forward. In fact, by the end of the Old Testament, mankind had successfully backed ourselves into the darkest corner of human existence—four hundred-plus years of silence.

Biblical scholar George Eldon Ladd described that period this way: "For centuries the living voice of prophecy had been stilled. No longer did God speak directly through a human voice to his people to declare his will, to interpret the reason for the oppression of Israel by the Gentiles, to condemn their sins, to call for national repentance, to assure judgment if repentance was not given and to promise deliverance when the nation responded."[1]

Thus the Old Testament's close marked a sad day in religious history. The cosmos had apparently lost contact with its deliverer.

Meanwhile, Israel gave piles of sacrifices, released endless scapegoats, partied hearty in who knows how many feasts—all to eventually turn their relationship with the Creator into a global board game. The board game, of course, was governed by power-hungry Pharisees who took it upon themselves to edit, expand, and enforce the rules at their every whim.

You can imagine the way their game unfolded: If you hang out with the wrong people, you lose. If you cut your hair wrong, you lose again. If you take one step too many away from home on the Sabbath, you triple-lose.

This was what religion had to offer the world.

And you think our religious institutions are disillusioning! Backtrack to when sacrificing a couple of pigeons—the crap-dispensing birds who waddle through the garbage of our current-day cities—was the best picture of salvation available to impoverished people whose sins needed forgiving.

There was no ultimate sacrifice, no Jesus, yet.

Needless to say, humanity was a disillusioningly long way from the garden community God had intended for us.

The New Testament temple, the religious institution of the day, was definitely no Eden. It was not an incubator where people came in contact with God. Rather, it was the headquarters of the people who ran the religious game.

It's no wonder Mr. Prepare the Way, aka John the Baptist, was a bit disillusioned. If I remember correctly, it was after flying off the handle and calling the religious leaders a "brood of vipers" that John then deleted the Hebrew family tree with one key stroke. Great-Great Grandpa Abraham or no Great-Great Grandpa Abraham, John said, the Israelites' religious leaders were ten seconds away from toast.

John the Baptist knew that what people were experiencing in the religious systems of their day was not what God intended. The Jewish temple system was not generating God's ideal for his community nor was it his final expression of involvement in the world.

Something greater was coming—a new revelation—which, given the tragic state of affairs, was why this information truly was "good news."

What would trump the religious systems was not another system, but a person!

A person named Jesus. And this Jesus immediately began doing the stuff of disillusioned people's dreams. He did away with institutionalized religion and instead championed a real-life faith where he hung out with his followers in a way that was perhaps a bit reminiscent of Eden. Jesus walked right alongside them, just like God had once walked in Adam and Eve's presence in the garden.

Through his teaching and example, Jesus shaped his friends into a community that merged the spiritual world with reality. In contrast to the temple, it was in the presence of Jesus and his followers that people would come in contact with God.

The community of people who followed Jesus and learned to live out his ideals was eventually deemed "the church." And here's some random trivia for you: the first guy to use the word *church* in reference to God's community of followers was also Jesus. In Matthew 16:18, Jesus called Peter the Rock on which he would build his church.

But here's the clincher. Jesus' exact words were: "And I tell you that you are Peter, and on this rock I will build my church, and the gates of Hades [or hell] will not overcome it" (NIV).

Don't you find it interesting that the very first time Jesus used the word *church*, he sensed the need to point out that hell cannot defeat it?

It's almost as if Jesus knew that the church was going to have a hard road ahead of it. That the church might sometimes look like it was going under.

But just to let you know ahead of time, Jesus said, it ain't gonna happen.

I've been thinking about this lately.

If Jesus told us from day one that the church was going to prevail—and if the church has already survived more than two thousand years of flaws since Peter began preaching his first sermons—I think it's possible that Jesus expected it to be a permanent fixture in human society.

This seems especially obvious in one of my favorite chapters in the Bible, John 17, where Jesus prayed for his disciples:

> My prayer is not for them alone. I pray also for those who will believe in me through their message, that all of them may be one, Father, just as you are in me and I am in you. May they also be in us so that the world may believe that you have sent me. I have given them the glory that you gave me, that they may be one as we are one: I in them and you in me. May they be brought to complete unity to let the world know that you sent me and have loved them even as you have loved me. (vv. 20–23, NIV)

Did you get that? Jesus prayed for those who would believe in God because of the message of his disciples. In other words, he prayed for us, the future church.

I don't know about you, but the fact that Jesus prayed for me—and for our generation of church—seems pretty significant. Significant enough to pay attention to his exact words.

And one of the things Jesus prayed was that his future followers may "be brought to complete unity" like the unity experienced between him and his Father.

Jesus' prayer was that we be unified with God and also with each other.

Jesus valued unity. Not only that, but did you catch what he said would result from such unity?

He said, "May they be brought to complete unity to let the world know that you sent me and have loved them even as you have loved me."

Letting the world know that Christ loves them through unity? Now that's a definition of church I think my generation can get behind.

I'm not exactly sure how this is going to work, but in light of some of my studies, I want you to know that I plan to stick with you, Church.

Discussion Questions

1. What do you think it would have been like to live before Jesus started the church? Do you think it would have been easier or harder?
2. From what you know about the Gospels, was Jesus' role as a reformer an easy one or did he experience some pain and difficulty along the way?
3. Does the fact that Jesus himself was the first person to bring up the idea of church impact its legitimacy in your mind?
4. Why do you think Jesus told Peter that the gates of hell would not prevail against his church?
5. When Jesus prayed for future believers, he said he hoped they would live in unity so that observers would understand

that God loved them. Why do you think unity communicates love? Do you think it is possible for the church to communicate love without it?

Key Observation

Because Jesus himself maintained that the church
was going to prevail, it is reasonable to suggest that the
church, in some form, will and should remain
a permanent fixture in society.

The Most Responsible Letter Yet

Dear Church,

I can only imagine how a few of my peers will respond to my last letter.

All right, then, I'm fine with championing the ideal of Christ, as long as you don't banish me back to the local church where I came from.

Ahhhh. This brings us back to our earlier debate: Should the disillusioned stick with their local congregations?

Again, good question.

Should I end this correspondence with a flight attendant-like spiel that points the disillusioned to their church's nearest emergency exit? Or should I encourage them to strap on their seat belts and learn to use their oxygen masks so they can weather more of their church's turbulent flights?

Neither option, of course, does my own experience justice.

If I suggest the disillusioned cut all ties to their local congregations, then I would risk hurting someone I love — you, Church. After all, it would be just a shade rude to write you all these letters just to announce that I am leading a campaign to destroy your local branches, don't you think?

However, telling the disillusioned to immediately return to their churches is advice my peers are no more likely to follow than kissing dating goodbye (a good idea, perhaps, but one a lot of people just aren't willing to buy).

If I blindly tell discouraged people to plug back in to their churches regardless of their circumstances, I would be foolishly failing to acknowledge the individual nature of each person's situation. Not to mention, I would be preserving my own hypocrisy in print for years to come because I would be giving out advice that I myself have not always been able or willing to follow.

The lack of a clear and clever answer, of course, is why I have avoided the question until now.

Not to mention that, to be honest, it's just not as simple or as entertaining to write about solutions to problems as it is to write about problems themselves.

It's frighteningly easy to criticize everything about the church right down to the royal blue choir robes that clash with the sanctuary's burgundy carpet. It's admittedly even a bit fun to rave about the freakish baptistry flowers that look like they came from Beetlejuice's botanical garden. And it's near-irresistibly tempting to question the church's many bizarre practices, like how we shrank the Lord's Supper into the world's tiniest combo meal that comes with one Chiclet-sized wafer and one nonrefillable thimbleful of Welch's.

But it's enormously difficult and not the least bit thrilling to do the opposite. To actually take the time to examine the source of a lot of my frustrations: not the church itself, but me.

It's nowhere near as humorous to face up to my own pain and frustration. To stare my emotions in the eye. To swallow hard and take apart my own complaints and inevitably see the less-than-glamorous things they tell me about myself.

Like the fact that I'm impossibly impatient. That I'm critical. That I lack stamina. That I am biased. That even my judgments about the local church are as flawed and messed up as the local church itself.

I could go on. (But why would I want to?)

And, it's equally unattractive to throw this "buck up and grow up" message in the face of the disillusioned. I might as well toss my toothpick body to a pack of ravenous wolves.

Given the difficult nature of the church-attendance question and the intensity of the potential responses, I fear I can't dive into this dilemma with my usual flippancy and sarcasm. And so, with great sadness, I must give up some of my appealing cynic's charm and write a letter that is decidedly wiser and more responsible than some of my previous rants.

I know. Wise and responsible. Woohoo! Sounds exciting, doesn't it?

Besides, in light of my previous rants, some of you might doubt that I *have the ability* to write a letter that is wise and responsible.

Yeah, well ... time will tell, yes?

Should the disillusioned return to their local congregations? I am going to begin by offering an extremely qualified no.

No? I can hear your protests above my typing. *Hey, I thought you said this was going to be a responsible letter! Saying people don't necessarily need to return to their congregations does not sound very responsible.*

But that's why I said it's an *extremely qualified no.*

I do think, in time, some of the church's missing will go back to regular weekend services at their local congregations. But for the time being, I am less concerned with whether or not we earn the perfect attendance award in Sunday school and more concerned that we move beyond disillusionment and engage the mission of the church.

See, I just can't bring myself to say, "Yes, you should all definitely return to your churches," because, first of all, I don't think it's fair to ask people to bow to the wishes of some stranger who just happens to have a good enough command of the alphabet to throw together a few letters.

I am a firm believer, on the other hand, that God has a relationship with *individuals* for a reason. So, my disillusioned friends, rather than pretend that I am your very own personal prophet and issue a largely uninformed blanket statement encouraging all of you to go back to your original places of worship,

I am going to encourage you to really dig deep and seek God's answers for your situations for yourselves.

Besides, even though I lean heavily toward the ideal of church, in rare cases I have to acknowledge *some* church contexts *can* be genuinely stifling and unhealthy. Or, at least, they can be repressing for people with certain types of gifts or dreams that may not be welcomed by their boards or congregations. And I also have to concede that God sometimes plants a vision in a person's heart that would best thrive somewhere other than the local church he or she is currently attending. (Some visions might be better suited for a larger or smaller city, a remote rural area, or even overseas, for instance.)

Now it's the disillusioned who are sighing in relief. *Good, because if you would have insisted I go back, I would have had to introduce your book to the garbage disposal.*

Well, gang, you may want to leave your paper shredder running because, as I noted earlier, this is an uncharacteristically *responsible* letter. Which means I have to say and ask things that are responsible, such as "Is leaving the church the *only* sensible response to disillusionment? Or are there other ways we could react to our disappointments?"

Just to give a shout out to the generation before us, I'm going to throw back to a linear format for this one and ask you to examine four — yes, exactly four — possible responses to disillusionment.

(While the boomers wearing their wisdom in their hair take notes on the four points, you twentysomethings can try to figure out if there are actually seven or maybe three million alternative responses or if, perhaps, you can condense all four into one. I am not attached to the number four. I'm just trying to make sense.)

In response to disillusionment, I would like to humbly suggest — based on my own experience — that you can choose to:

1. Say bon voyage to your local congregation and set out in search of a new one,
2. Velcro yourself back to the local congregation you came from and press on even harder,

3. Start some type of alternative Christian community with your wild and crazy like-minded friends, or

4. Give up on community altogether and roam around the world like a raving lunatic who is so compulsively opinionated that he can't find a single person who agrees with his position in life.

As you may be able to guess, option four is *not* my top recommendation. But we'll get to that. Let's take them one at a time. In this letter, I should have time to get to the first option: leaving your local church.

Don't get me wrong. I don't think that God intended for there to be locks on the church doors and bars on the church windows, but I do suggest that we use *extreme* caution when exiting our local congregations. (Did you catch that? *Extreme caution.* That sounds wise and responsible, doesn't it?)

It's one thing, for example, to leave a local congregation because we move away to college or take a job in another state, but leaving a local congregation for any other reason requires large amounts of prayer.

Of course, hearing God's direction is not always as clear as the PA announcing the sale on Cap'n Crunch at the local grocery store. So how does one determine what God's desires are for his or her specific situation?

Let's start with the voice of the Holy Spirit.

Ahhhh, the infamous voice of the Holy Spirit.

Whatever you do, don't picture some eerie apparition floating in and out of your soul. I'm not talking Casper the Friendly Ghost's spiritual twin. I'm talking the companion-Spirit that Jesus left to internally prompt us in the right direction.

For instance, when you pray about your situation, do you feel unresolved anger toward certain people in your local church; that bailing would prove something to someone? Do you sense that leaving the church would be running away from a problem instead of facing it?

I'm no prophet when it comes to deciphering the role of the Holy Spirit in our lives. However, I do know the difference between a good feeling and a terrible feeling. I know the difference between feeling free and lighthearted, like I *should* or at least *could* leave a church in good conscience, and the feeling that strangles my diaphragm and threatens my oxygen supply if I so much as inch toward the church door. (They call this the gift of discernment, I think.)

If we pray and *still* can't tell if God is pushing us one way or another, then, by all means we can continue seeking further wisdom regarding our church attendance. But if our stomachs are trying to wrestle themselves out of giant square knots, maybe we need to think further about the work God might have left for us to do inside our local churches.

Yeah, I know. Not necessarily the advice you were looking for. Sorry. That's how this wise and responsible thing works sometimes.

But if your conscience *doesn't* have you in a choke hold, how do you continue investigating whether it is okay to leave your local church?

I can think of a pretty obvious next step. But since I know you're probably all over this already, I'll just insert a brief paragraph as a reminder of sorts.

It is very unlikely that God would ask us to do something that goes against any truth expressed in the Bible. So, if in leaving our local congregations, we would commit some sort of scriptural infraction, like acting in pride or causing our brothers and sisters to stumble, that should make us think twice.

After seeking God through prayer and filtering our decision through the truths of Scripture, we could always pursue the advice route as well. And while I don't think Dr. Phil is going to do an episode on leaving the church any time soon, there's always a chance some of our mentors or peers might have something worthy to say on the subject of our church attendance. That is, if we just stopped complaining long enough to hear them.

Let me specify that I mean *Christian* mentors or peers, folks who are committed to God's vision for our lives. In order for them to be a true safeguard, they must know us well enough to understand the demands of our daily routines and have had the chance to observe our behavior patterns in a variety of situations. It helps if they have the guts to be honest too.

If our peers say things like, "I really respect the way you've handled yourself with this church thing and I think it is clear that God is directing you to a new place," then the bell rings and hallelujah, brother or sister, you win. Move on. However, if they point out issues that you still need to resolve, then sorry, you have to move back three spaces and at least give good old-fashioned resolution a shot. (Granted, God may sometimes move us on in a way our peers can't readily understand, but in general, it is probably a good idea to listen closely to their warnings.)

After our immediate mentors and peers, it can't hurt to seek the affirmation of the larger Christian community. In fact, Christians outside of our local congregation may offer the *most* objective counsel because they are not tangled up in our local church's situation.

For instance, as I wrote these letters, I was particularly aware of the need to hear the advice of diverse groups within the larger Christian community. Hence, I talked to my Southern Baptist church-planting father, my emergent nondenominational church staffers, my contemplative pastor friend, a former foreign missionary, my Free Methodist college chaplain, my university's Quaker vice president and president, my mystic-loving mentor, my former speech professor ... and the list goes on.

While seeking their input, I not only got to hear a wide sampling of perspectives, but because most of them are older than me, I also got to tune into an especially precious voice: the voice of experience.

Sometimes I think that nothing better illustrates the beauty of Christ's intergenerational following than the wisdom discovered when a young person's ideas about the church collide with the ideas of our parents' or grandparents' generation. The church of yesterday won't let us rush too far ahead, but the church of tomorrow won't let us stay where we are. We, like America's political system, have to constantly examine opposing perspectives and find a way to cooperatively evolve, to improve our character and to bolster our weaknesses in order to help balance the church of the future.

Lastly, after listening closely to the larger Christian community, I suggest we might be able to pick up a thing or two from studying Christian tradition. You wouldn't believe some of the things the church has fought over and held councils over and killed people over! Reading a little bit of the old history books can help put your current dilemma into better focus.

Somehow, realizing that people were tied to stakes and lit on fire for believing in a personal relationship with God makes your church's failure to acknowledge your birthday in the bulletin seem less of an offense.

If you make it through these booby traps — prayer, the Bible, the advice of peers, your larger Christian community — and still feel that God is redirecting you to a new church, I would lastly suggest that before you exit your existing congregation, you commit to doing the following:

Confirm that, to whatever extent you are able, you have genuinely tried to work toward a solution to any concerns you might have. Please don't forget to investigate the possibility that God could be using your concerns as an opportunity for you to strengthen the weaknesses in the church you currently attend.

Formulate a plan for where and how you will continue to experience community if you leave your church. Map out resources that will help replace the benefits of Christian community you will lose in the process. How will you engage the Bible, express worship, experience life-on-life learning, live in accountability, draw inspiration, employ your spiritual gifts, and soak up leadership training? In other words, don't dive into the ocean without a boat. And don't launch out in a boat unless you know how to sail one.

Determine, if possible, to wisely time your departure by not pulling out in a way that will further harm the church. If you have three months to go in your term as Director of Everything that Holds the Church Together, for instance, you might want to wait ninety days before you leave.

Review what living in the tension between "what is" and "what should be" may have taught you. There's no sense in learning a hard lesson twice. Some uphill battles are worth the strain, thanks to the endurance and courage they build in you and in others as well. Remember the truths you have discovered during this journey; instant message them on the screens of your heart, so that you will not lose them.

If at all possible, embark on your departure with a mutual exchange of blessings. When I left my staff position at my local church, I sat down and looked my pastor in the eyes and said, "For all the good and bad, I am not willing to leave here without giving you my blessing and receiving yours in return." Because of this intentional effort to stay teamed in our global cause even in my local resignation, this pastor remains a friend and valuable resource in my ongoing spiritual formation to this day.

I firmly believe that we best usher in our most ideal future when we make peace with and own the lessons of our past. And I lament the hardships that many encounter when they march forward without learning to bless those they have been teamed with in the past. This inability to find unity creates unfortunate chapters in the church's history.

Acknowledge that God might have something different in store for your local church than he has for you. The time may come when what God is stirring in you might be entirely different than the priorities your church identifies for itself. Rather than assume they've lost the beat of the Spirit's rhythm, I've learned to accept that God might be showing them something different than he is showing me. (That, as it turns out, is how God gets done more than one thing in the world at a time.) Besides, I am not responsible for what every other person does with their followership of Jesus. I am just responsible for what I do with mine. If I determine that because of my own passions I cannot stand with a local church's specific agenda, I also resolve that I will not stand against them.

State your ongoing love and support for the church and your desire to continue to share in community with this particular congregation. A good measure of health would be that you could return to attend a service as often as you like and still be welcomed.

Don't drag anyone's name or ideas through the mud on your way out the door. Whew. This is a hard lesson to learn, but a valuable one. Odds are, the average person in the congregation is not going to understand the intricate details of why your desires can't be accomplished in their local church. Giving them reason to criticize people or things that wouldn't normally be on their radar is a very sketchy decision. It can decrease their ability to respect, receive from, and be grown by their local church. And whether your local church is hitting your groove or not, God is still working there, continuing what he started. You wouldn't want to take away from that, would you?

All of that said, let me wrap up our discussion on leaving local churches by saying this: honestly, I really hope you don't end up leaving them.

I hope you won't have to leave your churches, I mean. I hope you'll find a way to be the kind of church God wants you to be inside your local church.

So until the next letter, here's hoping.

Discussion Questions

1. Why do you think it is easier to discuss problems in the church than it is to discuss solutions?

2. The author suggests that we at least attempt to resolve our concerns with the church we currently attend. What are some ways a person could go about doing this?

3. If someone asked you if it was okay to leave his or her local church, what would you say? Do you agree or disagree with the author's advice to people in this situation? Explain.

4. If people decide to leave their churches, the author asks them to do so only after in-depth consideration. Which of these considerations, if any, strikes you as especially important?

5. What are some lessons that you have learned while attending a church that was not exactly what you thought it should be?

6. What are some good things that God is doing in your local church that indicate he is still at work in this congregation?

Key Observation

Those who become disillusioned with the church should recognize that leaving it is only one method for dealing with disappointment. It would be wise to explore alternative solutions first, and then if we still choose to leave, to leave on the best terms possible.

Church at Home, Church on the Road

Dear Church,

Whew. Enough already about leaving our churches! What do you say we spend a while talking about the possibility of going back to the local churches we may have left?

I first considered the option of deepening my investment in the church, rather than withdrawing it, almost by accident.

During a conversation with my pastor, Ron Martoia, I told him that after college I intended to shift my efforts away from the church to the nonprofit sector (which to me seemed more focused on engaging *all* people).

Ron's response? "Sarah, I hear your dissatisfaction, but no matter what your grievance is, the church remains *the* institution that Christ himself appointed to carry his hope to the world."

Ron is a very smart man. However, despite the validity of Ron's reminder, my idealism was not easily distracted. "Well then," I countered, "show me the church that will engage these people and I will show you the church where I'll invest my life."

I said it almost facetiously, as a tongue-in-cheek challenge to a friend, but the idea stuck in my mind.

Then, seriousness dawned. *Huh. This is another option.* If my local church was willing, I realized, perhaps I could help lead the charge in recovering some of the values I felt were underrepresented in our congregation.

Several years and many hard conversations later, Ron hired me to be the director of Reach—the first official outreach-oriented arm of our church.

By giving me the chance to take ownership in its direction, this local church helped prevent me from walking away from the church at large. It made me a true partner in its mission. And it allowed me time to understand the value of Christian community well enough that I would never want to live without it.

I can't help but wonder if that's what my generation and some of the other disillusioned groups want too. Local churches that will allow us to take ownership in where the global church is going. Churches that will let us be true partners in determining how to carry out Christ's mission to our world.

If this sounds good to you, if you are looking for new ways to contribute to God's global mission through your local church, then, here are a few of my sometimes hard-learned suggestions:

Be honest about your feelings from the start. Let people help you find solutions that will make you stay. By quietly brooding over your concerns, you may plant seeds of pent-up anger or frustration that will eventually surface in ways that won't help your cause. Get to the point as early as you can and focus not on the problem, but on the solution. A good way to engage the discussion might be, "I have really enjoyed my experience at this church. I've been thinking about this particular area of ministry and I think it would be a good fit here because it is a little bit different than some of our other ministries."

Don't think you have all the answers. This is an unadmirable tendency among Christian groups of which I confess I have been part. We like to read the latest books or hear the latest speakers and think to ourselves: *This person has discovered the way that God intended for his church to function.* We turn people's ideas into crazes that everybody-who-is-anybody must implement to be "cutting edge."

Maybe this is because it is just easier to declare we have *the* answer than to go on day after day only gradually growing toward greater understanding.

But as I write, I humbly remind myself and you, Church: God didn't give the answers to all the questions to any one person or any one generation. He is not about to give them all to me or my generation either. He purposely lets us enjoy the ups and downs of our lives, to endure the swings of the pendulum, to wade in the ebb and flow, to exhaust ourselves in the struggle to achieve balance. This tension between who we are and who we are striving to become is what keeps us active in the faith.

I am learning to take seriously the advice of Glenn Tinder, author of *Political Thinking*, who writes: "Do not try to arrive at ideas that no one has ever thought before. Not many of even the greatest thinkers have done that. The aim of thinking is to discover ideas that pull together one's world, and thus one's being, not to give birth to unprecedented conceptions. An idea is your own if it has grown by your own efforts and is rooted in your own emotions and experience, even though you may have received the seeds from someone else and even though the idea may be very much like ideas held by many others."[1]

Resolve to take whatever opportunities God presents you, regardless of size. If your dream opportunity doesn't present itself, take whatever opportunities do arise. Before I ever was given my outreach post at Westwinds, for example, I led an outreach-oriented small group and led a volunteer relief trip while overseeing the church's children's ministry. Both of these were ways of being faithful to what God was doing in my spirit as I waited, albeit impatiently, for bigger opportunities. Likewise, when I left my staff position at Westwinds, I continued to try to take small opportunities to be active in the global outreach arena. Because I was no longer employed by a church, I decided one small thing I could do was begin to post articles on the Web that could assist churches in doing the kinds of things I was passionate about. In the process, I stumbled onto an opportunity to share my ideas on a larger scale through Zondervan.

Don't rush it. Maybe God is showing you a small glimpse of a bigger opportunity that he will bring into play down the road. If things aren't moving ahead as fast as you wish, take time to prepare yourself for what you think God wants to do through you in the future. Get a degree or additional training; learn to articulate the importance of your ministry idea using solid, biblical evidence; fine-tune your organizational skills. There is a lot you can do before you actually *do*.

In encouraging people to reengage your local congregations, Church, I'd like to leave you with the same challenge I voiced to my friend Ron: Show us the church that will engage our concerns and we will show you the church where coming generations will invest their lives.

I mean this to be less threat and more reference to reality, but if you don't help us engage our concerns in your churches, I think there's a good chance that many in my generation will find ways to invest our lives engaging our concerns elsewhere.

« »

This leads me to a third option for responding to disillusionment: starting some type of alternative Christian community other than your local church.

From my observations, a good way to start a new community—whether it be small-group oriented, neighborhood based, nonprofit centered, or whatever else you can think of—is to invite a group of similarly passioned, somewhat like-minded people to pray and study God's ideals together.

This is how my dad's current church got started. While he was a pastor at one church, God gave him the opportunity to get involved in a home Bible study elsewhere in the region. The Bible study was just that—a Bible study. There was no stated invitation to join a church or to spearhead any new, permanent Christian community. The people who attended just hung out together and jointly explored what God was doing in their lives. Left in God's hands, it wasn't long before some of the ideas gained incredible momentum and a church was born.

Now, if you drive down Lewis Avenue in Ida, Michigan, you will see a local church where a cornfield used to be.

To this day, whenever I stand in this building that my dad's church attenders helped to build; whenever I walk around the property that we prayed over long before the Department of Natural Resources ever said the land was buildable, a powerful realization consumes me.

Because my dad and a group of like-minded people pursued what God was doing in their spirits, one more branch of God's global church, representing Christ's ideals to our world, took root. There was one more place that unashamedly marked itself as the home of Christian community—where people might see the spiritual and earthly worlds merge. Where people could come in contact with Jesus.

I smile to myself at this realization every time it recurs to me. Because of my dad's and others' faith, Ida has a little less corn but hopefully a lot more Jesus.

Along these lines, I offer you some of my own learnings:

Don't pressure yourself to stay for the wrong reasons. While I have been careful to discourage people from leaving a church for the wrong reason, I also have to acknowledge that it can be easy to stay at your local church for the wrong reasons. You can be tempted to stay because of familiarity, nostalgia, or even to prove a point. But all of these reasons will result in less satisfaction, less blessing, and less gain for the kingdom than doing what God wants you to do.

If you are seeking familiarity and comfort, let me remind you that you will never be safer than when you are pursuing what God desires. If you grieve the loss of your former memories, let me assure you that your memories will grow even sweeter when you realize how they have prepared you for God's new tasks in your life. And, lastly, though I don't think we should strive to prove a point to anyone in our former congregations, you can rest assured that when God is really moving in you, over the long term, you will not have to prove it to anyone. People will notice.

Don't give your life to a movement other than Jesus' mission. There are all kinds of "good" causes in the world, but there is only one cause that trumps all the rest—and that is the cause of Christ. Don't get sucked into religious movements that seem to be fueled only by a desire to be different or cool. Learn from and appreciate movements that are driven by a desire to know Christ, to be like him, and to be faithful to his mission.

Similarly, if a movement seems to churn out disciples who are chronic complainers, if they produce leaders who live to bask in the spotlight, if they leave their converts drifting in an open sea of relativism, then be suspicious. Converts to the church are not perfect. But if movements are grounded in God's aims, then their common bond should be that their disciples are morphing into people who look, smell, sound, and taste increasingly more like Jesus.

Be faithful to notice the signals God is prompting in you. Do you have some far-out-there vision? Does this idea keep recurring to you, no matter how you try to push it out of your mind? Over time, do you feel an increasing push to actually act on your idea? Do you even feel that by *not* moving on it you could possibly be *disobeying* God? Then, tune in. This *might* be God.

Wait for a support system. Having people with diverse gifts—teaching, administrative, and hospitality talents, for example—always bolsters the health of any group or organization. Though I don't think it's always necessary, it usually makes sense to wait to advertise your ministry until you actually have people to help lead your new initiative! If God blesses, and thirty or a hundred people join you right away, you'll likely want some support to be able to wisely steward the opportunity he has given you.

If no one arises to help you lead this initiative, you might want to consider whether it is really the right time to push ahead. If you still feel that God is prompting you onward, consider gaining necessary support by finding a local church or organization to mentor you or—if that is not available—establishing a board of advisors that can assist you along the way.

Also, don't rule out coming alongside a person or group already doing something closely related to what you have in mind. Joining someone else further along in the journey gives you a chance to learn on the job and puts you in contact with networks of people who may be similarly passioned. Time spent cooperating with an existing ministry might save you years of mistakes and setbacks if and when God gives you a leadership post in a similar venue in the future.

Be open to many different possible outcomes. If you start a small group to pursue your ideas and it becomes a *really* small group—even the world's smallest small group—and all you accomplish is growing a few people with similar passions, you still haven't wasted any time or effort.

After college, our best man—Wes—and a few of our friends moved into the south side of our city and engaged an idea they called The Plan. The Plan consisted of four people—Wes, Miguel, Tanya, and Nikki—who partnered with probably a dozen more people to build relationships with our city's diverse people groups while living in two side-by-side urban apartments. Over time, they hoped to all move on and serve in some major urban area together.

Unfortunately, or maybe fortunately, depending on how you look at it, the foursome and their friends didn't end up staying together for the long run. But while their teaming didn't result in the four of them together serving God in *a* city, it *did* result in them serving God separately in four different cities.

Right now, as I type this, Wes is in Boston, Tanya is in New York, Miguel is in Philadelphia, and Nikki is in Chicago. You tell me whether God's purposes were served by their one-time grouping in Jackson, Michigan.

Live life large. If you still feel uncertain about stepping away from the comfortable, you might want to begin with some small-scale initiatives that fall in line with your bigger vision. Admit to God that you are scared of full-on pursuing your biggest ideas, but pledge that you want to be obedient to follow him if he is trying to prompt you in bigger directions. Ask that as you take a step forward, he will give you further clarity about whether to continue.

Once it becomes apparent that God is doing something new in you, celebrate, but more than anything—go after it! Give it absolutely everything you've got. There is no better experience than letting God use your personal journey to do his work in others.

Expect the transition to be difficult. The grass may seem greener on the other side of your local congregation's fence, but a lot of times that is just the sun getting in your eyes. The biggest difference between attending someone else's church and starting your own version of Christian community is that you are now no longer the complainer, but the one who people complain to. Welcome to the world of your former church staff.

Resist mediocrity and, if possible, realism. Inevitably, people will tell you that you are too idealistic. They will tell you that you are a dreamer who doesn't quite understand the way the real world works. Feel free to take that as a compliment that you *still have faith* that God can transcend the real world. Then, be smart and alert, but keep moving. Hanging around in stagnant water only makes you more susceptible to disease.

Protect your health. A lesson I learned early on that I have confidently repeated to everyone I know is this: Christians should err on the side of health. Err on the side of doing too much to exercise your head, heart, and spirit. Err on the side of too much accountability, of holding yourself to a higher standard than necessary, of putting boundaries in place that may sometimes restrict you. Err on the side of hearing warnings that surface along the way. Err on the side of not participating in behaviors that diminish your capacity to live your vision. Guard your ability to persevere at all costs. You will never feel worse than the day you have to give up opportunities to participate in God's mission because your spiritual health has been compromised.

When times get tough, ask God to make you tougher. When you hit a wall, don't you dare turn back. Borrow a crane or a bulldozer, build a makeshift battering ram, or pray for a tornado to tear down the wall. If you have to go and get a hammer and chisel away at that monster one centimeter at a time, pray that God will send you a lot of other people with hammers and chisels.

Put roadblocks on the road to quitting. Set aside regular time away from your mission to rest and regain your health so that you are strong enough to keep moving. Find an advisor to help you devise a plan to live your mission smarter, not harder. Call a friend who is impassioned enough to give you a pep talk and a helmet, then propel you right back into the wall headfirst. Perhaps the best thing you can do for your longevity is to purposely make it hard for yourself to quit.

Don't tie happiness to one specific outcome. It's not important that you instantly create a Christian community in which all your major concerns are addressed. What *is* important is that you attempt to respond to everything God shows you along the way. There's a chance that God will point you toward an outcome different than the one you were originally aiming for. Be willing to walk on an evolving path. If you insist on only pursuing your pet causes and concerns, you will be very disappointed to find that your version of church one day shows the same flaws as other congregations that once disillusioned you. Success is not being perfect, or even being more perfect than your previous churches. Success is being faithful to what God is doing in your life.

Maintain the mainline spiritual disciplines. In your rush to grab a spot on the nightly news as the most brilliant up-and-coming Christian community in your area, don't draw your new identity from forsaking your old one. Remember the practices — biblical teaching, discipleship, evangelism, prayer, worship — that made your former churches strong.

Stick together whenever possible. It would be wise if we twentysomethings learned to emphasize a deep respect for our spiritual parents; if we learned to vocalize that our faith has evolved thanks to many traditional churches and countless baby-boomer Christians; if we learned to crave the wisdom and blessing of the generations before us.

To my peers, then, I say this: If we work hard to maintain our relationship with the generations before us, I believe our older counterparts will faithfully put an arm around us and mentor us into our evolving leadership roles. This is not necessarily easy, as they sometimes have to mourn the loss of some of their traditions in order to guide us into our newly arriving shared future. Because the sad reality is, as cool as the generations before us are (and, I admit, I think they are pretty cool), logistically we can't do church the same as them. We don't have their exact background or skill sets. We don't see the world from their perspective.

But maybe it's okay that we are at least slightly dissimilar, because the methods that won awards in their generation may not be the favorite or most effective methods for ours.

My hope, then, is that other generations will read the statistics about twentysomething church attendance and spirituality and see more than just cold, clinical studies. I pray that they will look past the unoccupied rows at church and notice the vital signs that often only become evident by attaching a stethoscope to a real-live twentysomething. I pray that they will realize that the church of our generation *is* breathing, that our heart is beating, and that we need their help to complete our rite of passage in carrying the church toward tomorrow.

I beg of our seniors, come alongside us and help us see when we're operating too much in the gray zones; help us draw those important boundaries; help us understand the value of tradition. Encourage us to develop the characteristics we lack, so that we can take our identity as the church seriously. And if that means having to let us go to do our own thing, then, man, don't let us go without throwing a celebration that you have raised us to be so invested in the cause of Christ.

All that said, I come to the final option for responding to disillusionment with the church. And that is to start your own church with the average attendance of one. To wander aimlessly around your continent, unable to develop an alliance with a single person.

It's a joke! What good are you going to do the church if you're so jaded that you think you're the only one with the magic formula for getting church right?

If you aren't at a point where you can engage Christian community right now, that's okay. Take a break. But please, for the sake of your own well-being, keep an open mind to the possibility of engaging it somewhere down the road.

And be careful what you say, especially if something particularly tragic happened in your own church experience. Force yourself to acknowledge that not everyone's experience with church has been equally harmful. And realize that you may not be serving your own best interest or the interest of others by widely circulating every jaded thought that comes into your head.

Instead, be honest. There's nothing wrong with saying, "Hey, I realize that God wanted us to be a part of Christian community, but right now I am just too hurt and too frustrated to be able to function healthily in that setting. I'm not trying to sin or anything, but I need some time to really evaluate what I believe about organized religion. In the meantime, I would love to hang out with you, and you can rest assured I am not giving up on God or his desires for us anytime soon." Not only does this kind of confession promote understanding, it may help you build a support system. Perhaps the people who come around you in such moments will listen well and be your church in the moments when you choose not to attend a church building.

Lastly, I address the nondisillusioned or the people in current church leadership who are watching the rest of us sort through our options: Be of good cheer. There is a bright side to this process.

As Andy Stanley says, "Anyone who is emotionally involved—frustrated, brokenhearted, maybe even angry—about the way things are in the light of the way they believe things could be, is a candidate for vision. Visions form in the hearts of those who are dissatisfied with the status quo."[2]

If Andy is right, then my generation's tension may give way to vision. And if we are on the brink of birthing new vision, then there's a distinct possibility that you aren't dying on our watch after all, Church.

Perhaps you're just going through yet another stage of adolescence. A stage of adolescence that every generation of church attenders engages. I particularly like N. T. Wright's thoughts on this subject as he observes that "each generation has to wrestle afresh with the question of Jesus, not least its biblical roots if it is to be truly the church at all."[3]

So perhaps we should not resist the birth of this new vision, this re-creation. After all, every other living organism God created has the ability within it to procreate. Why should it be a surprise, then, that the church has a built-in reproductive system which allows it to birth movements that will attract new generations of Christ-followers?

Erwin McManus addresses this ongoing need for re-creation in his book *The Church in Emerging Culture*: "Jesus lives in every time and place in human history. He both makes himself known and manifests himself through the body of Christ. We should give up our role as preservationists — the church was never intended to be the Jewish version of the mummification of God. God is not lost in the past; he is active in the present. Our mandate is to continue the revolution Jesus Christ began 2,000 years ago."[4]

Continue the revolution? Now we're talking!

Perhaps twentysomethings will find something exciting in this church business after all.

Discussion Questions

1. When you consider your concerns with the church, which ones could you potentially help to solve?
2. If your church offered you the chance to do any kind of ministry you wanted, what kind of ministry would you want to do? Explain.
3. Even if you don't currently have any opportunities that you consider "huge," what small things might you be able to do to express what God is doing in your life?
4. What can you do to protect your health and stamina as you chase the visions God has placed in your spirit?
5. How have your generation's contributions changed the church today? What other changes do you believe your generation could contribute to improve the future church?

Key Observation

Disillusionment with the way things are
in the church can also inspire us to improve and
deepen our involvement in Christ's mission.

How Can We Go On Living?

Dear Church,

There comes a moment, after a particular bout of disappointment, when you begin to think that you are no longer fragile enough to have your life derailed by such deep disappointment again.

After all, you've owned up to a lot of your weaknesses, you've moved beyond most of your previous frustrations, and you've discovered ways to live toward solutions that will help repair the deficits you see in the church.

Somewhere along the way, you develop what you feel is especially thick, almost impenetrable skin.

You begin to think about disillusionment as an experience that happened a long time ago *before* you grew so significantly and started to see the world through a more mature lens.

Before you know it, you're operating as normal again. While you may not voice it aloud, subconsciously at least, you think the real cause for alarm has passed. You think the storm is over, that it is safe to just settle into run-of-the-mill ministry oblivion and casually live your identity as church once more.

Think again.

In an earlier letter, I compared disillusionment to a chronic illness because it has the ability to resurface out of nowhere.

That's what happened to me, anyway.

I worked through a lot of my concerns about how the church built or didn't build relationships with some of society's diverse people groups. I found the confidence to acknowledge and challenge instances from history and modern-day society where Christians seemed to misrepresent Christ's message. I learned to grow up and buck up and correct some of the ways I misrepresented Christ myself. All the while, I developed better research skills and an improved ability to articulate biblical and rational arguments to support my positions. And with help, I found some solutions that I was excited to invest in *for life*.

As a result, I thought that I had shaken free of most of my former frustrations.

If you would've asked me, I would have sighed in relief and told you that, thankfully, I had officially put my disillusionment to rest.

Unfortunately, however, life is not always what it seems.

Little did I know, for instance, that there was still a database in my mind that logged all the inconsistencies, flaws, and failures in the church's previous record. And although I had moved beyond consciously accessing that database in my regular routines, I found out that the database occasionally begins spitting out data all by itself.

If something bad enough happens, all those former anxieties and frustrations can be triggered by some automated mental process and restored to new life before you even realize what is happening.

My second case of noticeable, life-altering disillusionment unfolded like this, piercing my life in a surprising and entirely new way from disappointments past.

This time my distress was not just related to the global church's interactions with Chicago or even my own city's diverse people groups. It was not a distant disillusionment with a nameless, faceless church "system," and its victims were not groups of only recently discovered strangers.

This time, I encountered disillusionment in Christian communities that had names. And faces. In fact, a lot of faces. The names weren't just any names and the faces weren't just any faces either. This time the church bore familiar names—names that were entirely precious to me, names that I had strongly identified with, names that had come to represent so much that was good in the faith arena and in myself.

The faces were the faces of people I dearly loved.

In two back-to-back instances in my life, people who I related to, people who inspired me, people I *loved* were caught up in messy, hurtful church-related stories that awakened a new kind of grief in me.

Combined with my previous disillusionment—which now seemed even more valid than before—this fresh disappointment tragically skewed my perception of the church in ways I still haven't fully recovered from.

Suddenly, Christian community again became synonymous with pain. Walking into a church building—any church building—felt like getting repeatedly punched in the stomach until my body finally went into welcome shock and I became so numb that I didn't even care that I was being punched.

Ghosts from the past haunted my memories, ruining potentially positive experiences in the present. Ghosts from the future repressed my ability to dream, constantly reminding me that any vision—no matter how God-inspired, no matter what the level of commitment or talent—could fall apart at the seams as if it had never existed.

I remember one particular night, I began sobbing almost hysterically.

Similar to my life flashing before my eyes, my mind replayed all the people—those who I was personally connected to, those on the other side of the world, those from the pages of the history books—who had paid some sort of cost while involved in the work of the church.

And I just could not stop crying.

When my husband came in to investigate, I was unusually uncommunicative. All I remember repeating—over and over again—is, "It's too hard. It's just too hard."

Needless to say, I was an absolute mess.

I felt as though I had spent my entire young adult life living for an institution that wasn't worth living for. And now that my former optimism about church was shattered, I didn't know what causes—if any—remained worthy of my ongoing life investment.

You can perhaps best hear my renewed conflict about my involvement in the church by reading a few of the blogs I wrote at the time.

07.15.04

Admission. There are some days when I no longer want to be the church. I want to walk away. Call it quits.

Why the occasional urge to bail out the nearest emergency exit? Fear, grief, disappointment, anger. You name it. Even the best laid human intentions sometimes misevolve the church into a cannibalistic organization that eats its own leaders.

So lately, I weigh the cost, wondering, "How many times will I have to watch the lives of those I love be sacrificed?" Wondering, "How many times can I feel this level of grief before I lose the ability to see the cause as noble?"

And I choose to press on. Sometimes only because I know that outside of the church there lies even more devastation. That the hope she carries is our only shot. Without her, we've got nothing.

So I cross the line in the sand one more time and say: I will be the church. Sometimes that is all I can do.

« »

07.26.04

Sighhhhh. It's not easy being church.

I don't know about you, but everywhere I look, I see friends making heavy sacrifices for the kingdom.

And I'm not talking about foreign missionaries getting speared by hostile aborigines. I'm talking about sacrifices of the everyday variety. Little sacrifices that occur as we try to balance ministry initiatives and family; the price paid each time we exhaust ourselves solving some divisive congregational drama. Small stuff can cost us big.

I remember the words of Paul and take comfort. "I will gladly spend and be completely spent for the sake of the church" (see 2 Cor. 12:15).

When it comes down to it, I guess we're all going to expend our energy, suffer mistakes, and endure pain doing something. If that's the case, then I'm glad we're choosing to make sacrifices for something that matters this much.

« »

08.17.04

I am frequently torn between two perspectives. On one hand, I earnestly want to invest my life in the global church. I want to live with a sense of expectation that God will complete each vision he started ... in my life and elsewhere.

Even in the midst of grief and tension, I want to speak from a deeply rooted, unwavering sense of hope.

The other part of me, however, wants to wave the white flag of sad acknowledgment. I want to give up the cause and admit that—no matter what I do—I cannot change the painful potential of my world.

I want to concede the irony of it all ... that if I wish to pursue God's kingdom here, I must step into the line of fire. If I want to help take the hill, I will have to watch my friends fall beside me and be wounded myself.

And despite all my ambition, I too will fail to fully carry out my good intentions. It seems we cannot pursue the good without tasting the bad. It rains on the just and unjust alike. "Frankly, this side of eternity we will never unravel the good from the bad, the pure from the impure," Richard Foster says. But he points out, "God is big enough to receive us with all our mixture. That is what grace means, and not only are we saved by it, we live by it as well."[1]

During the height of my disillusionment, following a morning worship service at the church where I had formerly worked, I fell into seemingly casual conversation with the wife of one of our church's elders. Janet, along with her husband, Jeff, had been attending our church over half my lifetime ... a commitment that, by itself, gave them credibility in my eyes.

Perhaps what I respect most about Janet and Jeff is that when I spoke with them about my own painful wrestling matches with the church at large, they did not try to casually explain away my concerns.

They were honest. Their experience with the global church had also been marked with bouts of hurtful disillusionment. On a couple of occasions, in fact, this disillusionment had severely diminished Janet's desire to attend or participate in local church community.

In one dark moment, when the weight of my concerns seemed particularly heavy, I posed this question to Janet through tears: "If the church is the hope of the world, then why would I go on hoping?"

(I can be a bit extreme sometimes, if you haven't noticed.)

Janet smiled sadly. "Sarah," she said, "don't let anyone mislead you. Sometimes leaders claim that the church is the hope of the world in an effort to help people understand their shared identity in Christ's mission. But the church is *not* the hope of the world. Jesus is."

And, of course, Janet was right.

Sometimes I think we must've read the Bible and our Marvel comic book back-to back and emerged with the impression that we are supposed to be superheroes who right all the world's wrongs.

Somewhere along the line, I had gradually bought into this logical fallacy as well. In my attempts to examine how I felt church *should be*, I had allowed too much of my faith to hinge on the humans who drove the institution.

But the Great Commission was not passed out with spandex suits or vinyl capes. And that, of course, is because we aren't the hope of the world. For Pete's sake, on our own we're not even the hope of Metropolis.

Through Janet's comments and the following months of reflection, I found the answer that closed the gap between what church was and what I believed church should be. His name is Jesus. Jesus is the matrix that makes it possible to see my world, and even my flawed religious institutions, in light of hope.

We Christians were never the hope. Yes, we were and are carriers of the hope. But we ourselves are only reflections — often dim reflections — of the hope we internalize: Jesus Christ.

One of my favorite theologians, N. T. Wright, says it this way. "We do not have to achieve what Jesus achieved; we cannot, and even to suppose that we might imitate him in that way would be to deny that he achieved what in fact he did. Rather — and this is absolutely crucial to understanding what is going on — our task is to implement his unique achievement."[2]

Whew. Big sigh of relief.

I guess we can stop exhausting ourselves trying to run faster than a speeding bullet, and let our muscles relax after all those buildings we've been jumping in single bounds.

Of course, in noting our nonsuperhero status, Church, I am not suggesting that you have *no* role to play and are thereby *exempt* from any action. Obviously, the church is *the* key earthly player in Christ's unfolding drama.

Paul underlines the critical importance of the church's role by suggesting that the church is an expression of Christ's fullness, although it is Christ who does the actual filling. He writes in Ephesians 1:22–23: "And God placed all things under his feet and appointed him to be head over everything for the church, which is his body, the fullness of him who fills everything in every way."

Although we are important, then, we should be careful of applauding ourselves too loudly. I notice that when we are taking our bows, we often let our importance go to our head. We sometimes think that we—with all our leadership insight—make or break the local church. We think that even the global church hinges on the success of a few standout local churches like ours, that are willing to lead the way.

But when we get carried away with our own role, Church, I've noticed that we often lose sight of our true identity within the mission. We begin thinking and acting as if *we* are the hope.

In effect, as Paul describes it in Colossians 2:18–19, we run around like a church that's lost its head: "Do not let anyone who delights in false humility and the worship of angels disqualify you. Such people also go into great detail about what they have seen, and their unspiritual minds puff them up with idle notions. They have lost connection with the head, from whom the whole body, supported and held together by its ligaments and sinews, grows as God causes it to grow."

But I can't be unduly hard on the current-day Christian institutions. We certainly are not the first to fail to live out our correct identity in the history of the church.

Unfortunately, the pages of the Bible are littered with examples of people who edited the roles God gave them to suit their own desires. This pattern is especially evident in the life of God's people during the time of the major prophets.

Isaiah tells us that the nation of Judah continually operated within a self-designed salvation: a little bit of God, a little bit of Eastern religion (Isaiah 2:6), a little bit of materialism (2:7), a little bit of power (2:7), and a display case full of handmade idol trinkets (2:8). They came to believe a lie: that they could derive more hope from their human-driven piecemeal religion than they could draw from God himself.

Judah's insistence on manufacturing their own version of hope did not serve them well, of course. It created an environment susceptible to spiritual sickness and eventually destruction at the hands of Assyria.

Jeremiah paints a very similar picture. Judah is now threatened by Babylon, but the nation doesn't respond with the urgency such a threat should generate. Rather than realign their allegiance to God, their true hope, they trust in a genetic insurance policy. *Because we're God's chosen people, we obviously can't be wiped out.*

But Jeremiah has a message for Judah, which in essence, can be summarized: "Wanna bet?" Jeremiah urges Judah not to rest in a false sense of security, thinking that they are safe because *they* are the true religion and the guardians of the temple. On the contrary, Jeremiah insists, they must internalize God's truth to have any real claim to hope.

With Isaiah and Jeremiah's books as background, it is Ezekiel—who writes during the Babylonian exile—who clinches the lesson for me, Church. And this time, those who are basing their religion on the connection to the temple have screwed up one better. This time, their sin—relying on what they deem to be a hopeful combination of idol and sun worship—has even permeated their place of worship (Ezekiel 8). They are literally keeping idols in secret rooms within the temple!

God's response may seem a bit surprising. He summons six warriors to slay everyone, including women and small children, who failed to rely on him.

Then, God goes one step further, Church. He commands the warriors to defile the temple by piling the city's dead bodies in its courts (which would have been a monstrous grievance according to laws concerning temple cleanliness). What follows is the deepest wound of Judah's judgment: God removes his glory from the temple.

Sometimes, Church, I just sit back and think about this illustration for hours.

I wonder ... ideally, how should Judah have responded to the message of the prophets?

Certainly, to revert to a hope founded in God alone would have been in order. But I also wonder, was God hoping that even one little priest would pull a Paul-Revere ride, screaming, "We are misled! We do not glean our hope from our building!"? I like to think, Church, that someone with more guts might've even cried out, "And let the sin-stained temple burn, God, because we know we don't need the temple. The temple is nothing, God. Our real hope is you."

And, I can't help wondering (and I truly am just wondering, not instructing), is it possible that, at times, God has acted or will act similarly toward later groupings of his people? Do we, like Israel, sometimes misunderstand our identity, believing that the institutional church—the collection of buildings—or we ourselves are the source of our hope?

To be honest, Church, I sometimes hear a lot of Israel in myself. When I asked Janet, "If the church is the hope of the world, then why would I go on hoping?" my attitude was not a far cry from Israel's reaction when they realized their temple had fallen.

In Ezekiel 33:10, Israel despairs, "Our offenses and sins weigh us down, and we are wasting away because of them. How then can we live?"

This, too, is what I wanted to know. *If the current church's offenses and sins weigh us down, and we are wasting away because of them, how then can we live?*

And this is where we are relieved to remember that our hope lies safely outside of ourselves and our religious institutions. God's response to Israel's cry, and to mine, is the ever-present happy ending after disillusionment.

"How then can we live?" Israel asks.

"As I live," says the Lord.

In tracking these ideas, I sense that there may be a connection between our disillusionment and how we sometimes mistakenly see ourselves.

Perhaps it is when we market ourselves as the hope of the world, or when we believe that other humans hold the hope of the world for us, without proper acknowledgment of Christ as our source, that we foster disillusionment.

But it is not our own ability to function perfectly that sustains our ministry efforts. It is only because God lives that we and our church can go on living.

And so it is with this return to God's sustaining life that this bout of my own disillusionment with you ends as well, Church. And it is with this affirmation that Jesus is the source of my hope that I will face whatever disillusionment is to come.

Because even if our sins do weigh us down, as they did ancient Israel, we cannot simply make room for them in our identities and spend our lives wasting away in them.

I believe that each bout of disillusionment—like all journeys—is eventually meant to come to an end.

How then, do we emerge from the darkness and renew our identity as God's church? How do we go on living?

"As I live," says the Lord.

Discussion Questions

1. Have you ever thought that you shook disillusionment only to have it return? What happened?
2. Have you ever fallen into the trap that the author describes by drawing hope from the humans who run the church?
3. People often feel like they can manipulate a better outcome than God. Have you ever tried to write an alternative plan to outdesign God? How did it work out?

The church is not the hope of the world; Jesus is.

Love Letters

Dear Church,

It may surprise you ... sometimes it surprises me ... that I am where I am today.

That I can still say I love you.

And, after all of this, you deserve one really good love letter.

It is difficult to describe how much I love you, but I once heard Bill Hybels take a pretty good stab at it.

Hybels was asked to speak at a church in Canada. Right before he took the stage, a woman from the congregation recounted her broken past — one that was characterized by hurt and disillusionment. Yet, her story had the ending of Hybels' dreams: she had been introduced to Jesus by that local church.

The woman's story melted Hybels. In his book, *Courageous Leadership*, he describes his internal response to her testimony: "You personify what my life is all about. I'd have given everything I am and have to hear one story like yours."

By the time he got to the stage, Hybels was an emotional mess. Abandoning his carefully planned speech, he opted to peel back his title and let people see straight into his heart. Right to his love for the church.

"Give your life to this.... Give all the money you can give. Give all the service you can give. Give all the prayers you can give. Give whatever you have to give, because for all eternity you'll look back over your shoulder and be glad you did."

Later, Hybels attempted to describe the depth of love he has for the church. "I can't count how many times I've fallen on my knees after a ministry event at Willow or elsewhere and said to God, 'Nothing else does this to me. Clearly I was born for this.'"[1]

And you know what, Church? Hybels' love for you does me in every time. When he describes his passion for local churches, every church-related moment of my lifetime swells to my memory and sends my heart into overdrive. I can't agree with him more. Being a member of your crew has been the premier privilege of my life as well. It's been that way as far back as I can remember.

So I write you, Church, because despite your flaws and despite my affair with disillusionment, I love you. Many of my peers love you too.

I love you because you are brilliant. You started out as this fragile little group of marginalized disciples that almost no one thought would succeed. Yet in a dot-comlike explosion, you emerged on the global scene as a force to be reckoned with. Google and eBay have nothing on you, Church.

I love you, Church, because you're accessible. From Philip's run-in with the Ethiopian to Peter's dream of animals falling from heaven, you refused to limit yourself to just one group of people. Now, missionaries from every country catapult themselves all over the world and back again just to make sure every tribe on the planet gets a personal invitation to join you. Sure, there are some barriers remaining, but I'm putting my money on you, Church. Forget McDonald's, you've served billions upon billions.

I love you, Church, because you're consistent. Dark Ages? You were there. Renaissance? You were there too. Enlightenment, modern, postmodern. There, there, and there. The US government may be determined to separate religion and the state, Church, but they've never figured out a way to teach history without mentioning you.

I love you, Church, because you take action. Despite entertaining Easter cantatas and mouthwatering potluck dishes, you aren't interested in the hotel business where people rent your rooms just to rest in comfort. No. You manage to punt people out into the community, as if you had forgotten that you ever had walls to keep them in. You reminded them, generation after generation, that Jesus' favorite verb was "go." Let's stay committed to revisiting this lesson as many times as necessary!

I love you, Church, because you're learning from your mistakes. Despite your role in the Crusades, your part in the abuse of Native Americans, or your failure to address American slavery, you kept trodding along until there were enough numbers among you to stand up for what was right. Despite cults who poisoned people with Kool-Aid, men who locked their followers in camps, and evangelists who slept around when the cameras weren't on, you carried your shame and regret without losing the ability to hold your head high.

I love you because you are tough. Fear could not bust up the commitment of your leaders. Lock them in prison? They'll write half the New Testament. Banish them to an island? They'll write the grand finale to the world's bestseller. Crucify them upside down? Their examples will become the rock upon which your future is built. Catacombs, hostile natives, guillotines, or guns to the head — the rusty, prickly gates of hell have heaved with all their force. But through the help of Jesus, your Head, you slammed shut the gates, proving again and again that hell would never prevail against you.

I love you, Church, because you're resilient. You've been portrayed from so many unflattering angles. Movies offer fanatical Christian characters trying to blow up government projects. TV shows present sweaty choir-robed mobs engaging in something akin to a pep assembly for exorcists. Comedians do gigs as kneesock-wearing Sunday school teachers with nasally voices and enormous bifocals. You've been laughed at, accused, ignored, and misused. But you always get up the next morning ready to press on toward the mark.

I love you, Church, because you're never satisfied with where you are. You revamp your music from psalms to chants to hymns to choruses. You move from contemporary to praise and worship ... and then, ironically, back to chants again. You always push yourself, examine yourself, try to improve yourself from generation to generation. I can't wait to see what you become in our generation.

I think more than anything, Church, I love you because of your flexibility. You started simple, known as little more than a group of friends who lived, ate, and prayed together.

You could have patented this idea, stamped this one model as *the* model—the only one you officially endorsed.

Yet, you let guys like Paul carry you around and disperse you all over the place. In Antioch, Iconium, Lystra, and Derbe. In prisons, synagogues, two-story houses, and courtrooms. You let common laborers such as Aquila and Priscilla conduct undercover church while doing everyday tasks like building tents. You took up root in the houses of ordinary people in Corinth, Galatia, Ephesus, Philippi, Colossae ... I could go on.

You met in stone buildings with dark, stained glass and columns that were operated by rabbis, monks, nuns, popes, and priests. You moved into brick buildings with high steeples and large wooden crosses. You lent yourself to vacation Bible schools, revivals, backyard Bible clubs, workshops, and conferences.

You exploded into buildings ten times the size of anything you'd lived in before, with huge digital screens and surround-sound stereo. You housed cutting-edge worship and emergent experiences right across the street from ones that practiced liturgical prayer and formal sacraments. You split yourself into cells, emergent villages, and then back to house churches. You hung out at faith-based nonprofits, coffeehouses, bars, and restaurants. And you topped it all off by becoming the world's first international corporation, popping up in cities, villages, and remote tribal outposts across the globe.

And if all of this were not enough, this part is hands-down what made me fall in love with you in the first place: you defied logic by transcending physical space. You showed the world that you didn't need steeples or crosses or truckloads of bricks. You set up residence in community itself, presenting yourself in the sometimes building-less "togetherness" of the Twelve and those who came after them. You *are* the community, even when the community only boasts two or three people.

I love you because I am part of you. Because when my friends and I are teamed in Christ's mission, we are you.

So, I write—first and foremost—because I love you.

I love you still. In fact, I somehow think I love you more.

There is something powerful about realizing that someone or something is not perfect and loving them anyway.

Sometimes, love is all the reason a person needs to stay in contact. So I leave you with this final message: I love you. Keep in touch.

Discussion Questions

1. If you had to stop right now and write a love letter to your local church (or the global one), could you do it? Explain.

2. If it would be difficult to write a love letter, is it because there is nothing to love, or because you've closed off space in your heart due to hurt and disillusionment? What might you do to release any lingering hurt or disappointment with the church and allow yourself to appreciate the positive contributions it has made and can make in your life?

3. If you would find it easy to write a love letter, how do you maintain a positive concept of the church while still acknowledging its flaws? Was there a stage of life when you grappled with forgiving your church? How did you get out of that stage?

4. If you don't feel that you can write a love letter to your local church, could you manage one for the global version? Are there Christians outside of your church who have influenced your life for the positive?

5. Share some of the things you love most about the church (be it local or global). List as many positives as you can. You may even want to compose your own letter to express your love for the community of people who follows Jesus in this world.

Key Observation

As with any close relationship, when we work through difficult stages with the church, we are likely to emerge with a stronger, more loving relationship.

One Last Thing

Dear Readers,

Thank you for taking the time to hear my reflections about the church at large.

As you were reading, I suspect you were tempted to respond to portions of these letters. Or, maybe you wanted to add some of your own experiences to mine by writing your own letter to the church. I would love to give you that chance! Please accept my invitation to post your own letters to me and to the rest of the church at *www.dearchurch.com*.

Also, if the contents of these letters seemed especially relevant to your church, I would love to come and hear your thoughts personally. I am available to join you in hosting an interactive service in your local community that centers on topics discussed in *Dear Church*. To make arrangements to have me visit your church, please contact me at sarah@dearchurch.com.

I look forward to hearing all you have to say.

Sarah

Acknowledgments

Special thanks to the following people who encouraged me to bring what God is doing in my life to expression:

Ben DeVries, who used one phone conversation and a handful of emails to convince me—a complete stranger—to capture this life stage in a book.

Angela, Greg, Rob, Michelle, Leslie, Scott, Joyce, and the others at Zondervan who not only edited, designed, and marketed this book, but often seemed to believe in its message as much or more than I did.

Westwinds' staff and elders—Norma, Amy, Cammie, Ed, Scott, Taryn, Trish, Dave, Kat, Andy, Jeff, Glenn, Rick, Denny, Craig, Lance, and Paul—for living and learning and never giving up during the highs and lows of real-life church. And blessings to the current and future Westwinds staff, who will seek God's future for this community together.

Westwinds' founding first family, the Martoia clan—Ron, Dad, Mom, Rick, Christina, Ryan, Collin, Justin, Val, RJ, Skyler, and Ari—who led, loved, and sacrificed deeply so that the story of Westwinds could be written in the Jackson community.

Desmond, Sam, Amanda, Jared, Shane, Melissa, Cassandra, Deeno, and other NexGeners who have evolved into some of my favorite fellow twentysomethings. You and your families have left a lasting impact on my life.

Spring Arbor University, New Life Tabernacle, Dundee Baptist Church, daVinci schools, the Vortex Learning Community, and CrazyHomeChurch.com for your investments and partnership in my life mission.

My grandparents—Roy and Marion Baker, Thomas and Betty Raymond, and Virginia Raymond—for laying a stable foundation for future generations of our family.

My extended family—my sister-in-law Melissa, the Raymonds, Harrises, and Hopples, along with the Cunninghams and Jenners—for their love and encouragement along the way. And James McNulty, who belongs in my definition of family as much or more than those who are genetically related. Thanks for the inspiration to look at life with fresh eyes.

Mary Darling and Tom Morrisey, along with countless Christian writers and bloggers who have lent their personality and influence to help me maximize this opportunity. Jane, Adam, Alex, Tony, Draven, Andrew, Tom, James, Matt, David, Amy, Sean, Rachel, John, Buzz, Michael, Paula, Tim, Dan, Peter, Jeff, Ken, Jan, Sal, Miller, Jason, Stacey, Brian, Jason, Rick, Bruce, Justin, Joel, Craig, Ryan, Jodi, Mark, Margaret, Dave, Gregg, and Fredrik—thanks for all your e-feedback that helped define the direction of this project.

Notes

Letter 1: Not Fine

1. "Twentysomethings Struggle," The Barna Group.
2. Bill Easum, "Strategic Mapping and Futuring," Easum, Bandy, and Associates: *www.easumbandy.com/resources/* (date posted unknown).
3. Gallup Poll, December 17–19, 2004, +/- 3% margin of error, sample size = 1,002 as found at *www.gallup.com/poll/content/default.aspx?ci=14446* on December 23, 2004.
4. Robert E. Webber, *The Younger Evangelicals* (Grand Rapids, Mich.: Baker, 2002), 48.
5. Dave Tomlinson, *The Post-Evangelical* (Grand Rapids, Mich.: Zondervan, 2003), 24.
6. Edgar C. Whisenant, *88 Reasons Why the Rapture Is in 1988* (Little Rock, Ark.: self-published, 1988).
7. "Generation Y," *Wikipedia: en.wikipedia.org/wiki/Generation_Y* (referenced September 25, 2005).
8. Tim Stafford, "The Church—Why Bother?" *Christianity Today*, January 2005, 44.

Letter 2: A Fine-Looking Group

1. Neil Howe and William Strauss, *Millennials Rising: The Next Generation* (New York: Vintage, 2000), 4.
2. Robert E. Webber, *The Younger Evangelicals*, 157.
3. "Boomers Lead Generation Giving, But Younger Groups Showing Potential," Association of Fundraising Professionals: *www.afpnet.org/ka/ka3.cfm?content_item_id=21989&folder_id=2345* (September 2005).
4. Peg Tyre, "Bringing Up Adultolescents," *Newsweek*, March 25, 2005, *www.hyper-parenting.com/newsweek5.htm*.
5. "Ideological Crossroads: Gen X Marks the Spot," The Gallup Organization: *www.gallup.com* (September 2003).
6. Ibid.
7. Gerald Schlabach, *And Who Is My Neighbor?* (Scottdale, Pa.: Herald Press, 1990), 17.
8. Joseph Heath and Andrew Potter, *Nation of Rebels: Why Counterculture Became Consumer Culture* (New York: Harper Collins 2004), 10.

9. "Generation Gaps in the Workplace," CNBC: *msnbc.com/id/3072412/* (August 29, 2003).

10. Eric Chester, *Employing Generation Why* (Lakewood, Colo.: Tucker House, 2002), 13.

11. Susan Dominus, "The Mysterious Disappearance of Young Pro-Choice Women," *Glamour*, August 2005, 201.

12. "The Cubicle Can Wait for an Adventure or Two!" *Delaying the Real World: www.delayingtherealworld.com* (2005).

13. Lisa Belkin, "Psst, New Grad. Put the Career Off." *New York Times: www.nytimes.com/2005/05/22/jobs/22wcol.html?ex=1121918400&en=a96 64ef1196029d3&ei=5070&emc=eta1* (May 22, 2005).

14. "Twentysomethings: Coming of Age in the Age of Responsibility," *Portico Research: www.porticoresearch.com/2125.html* (2002).

15. Randall S. Hansen, "Navigating the Quarterlife Crisis to Career and Personal Success," *Quintessential Careers: www.quintcareers.com/quarter life_career_crisis.html* (date posted unknown).

16. "HELP Committee Chairman Enzi to Advance JOBS Initiative with Education, Workplace Safety Bills." *Office of the Senator Michael B. Enzi: http://enzi.senate.gov/helpjobs.htm* (April 12, 2005).

17. Craig Dunham, "Motivating Twentysomethings. They're Here — Now What?" *Group's Church Volunteer Central: shop.grouppublishing.com/cvc/in side_track/issue_5/motivation.html* (July, 2005).

18. Brian McCollum, "Full Transcript of Eminem Interview," *Detroit Free Press: www.freep.com/entertainment/music/emfull30_20000630.htm* (June 30, 2002).

19. Ben Ferguson, *It's My America Too* (New York: William Morrow, 2004).

20. "The Ben Ferguson Show," *Radio America: www.radioamerica.org/ Program2003/benferguson-interview.htm* (2003).

21. "Ben Ferguson: America's Youngest Nationally Syndicated Talk Show Host," *Premiere Speakers: premierespeakers.com/3439/index.cfm* (2004).

22. Ibid.

23. *Images of Singles and Young Adults: SAM Journal: www.cookministries.com/ events/sam_journal/index.cfm?N=25,94,4,2* (July 2005).

24. Eric Chester, *Employing Generation Why*, 24.

25. Roger Putnam, *Bowling Alone* (New York: Simon and Schuster, 2000), 133.

26. *www.cdc.gov/nchs/pressroom/02news/ameriwomen.htm*

27. Steve Finlay, "Why Toyota Wants Gen Y," *Keep Media: www.keepmedia. com/pubs/WardsDealerBusiness/* (January 1, 2003).

28. "Generation Y Goes Shopping," *Chief Marketer: http://chiefmarketer.com/ crm_loop/database/gen-y-071405* (accessed February 25, 2006).

Letter 3: No Gatekeepers

1. "People: Race and Ethnicity," *U.S. Census Bureau: factfinder.census.gov/ jsp/saff/SAFFInfo.jsp?_pageId=tp9_race_ethnicity* (last revised October 13, 2004).
2. "People: Origins and Language," *U.S. Census Bureau: factfinder.census. gov/jsp/saff/SAFFInfo.jsp?_pageId=tp7_origins_language* (last revised August 27, 2004).
3. "QT-P17. Ability to Speak English: 2000," *U.S. Census Bureau: factfinder. census.gov/jsp/saff/SAFFInfo.jsp?_pageId=tp7_origins_language* (2000).
4. "People: Relationships," *U.S. Census Bureau: factfinder.census.gov/jsp/saff/ SAFFInfo.jsp?_pageId=tp10_relationships* (last revised October 12, 2004).
5. "People: Disability," *U.S. Census Bureau: factfinder.census.gov/jsp/saff/ SAFFInfo.jsp?_pageId=tp4_disability* (last revised August 2, 2005).
6. "QT-P17. Ability to Speak English: 2000," *U.S. Census Bureau.*
7. "People: Education," *U.S. Census Bureau: factfinder.census.gov/jsp/saff/ SAFFInfo.jsp?_pageId=tp5_education* (last updated January 19, 2005).
8. "QT-P32. Income Distribution in 1999 of Households and Families: 2000," *U.S. Census Bureau: www.census.gov* (2000).
9. "People: Race and Ethnicity," *U.S. Census Bureau.*
10. Marilyn Brenden, "Ministering to Missing Class Members," *The Clergy Journal: www.findarticles.com/p/articles/mi_qa3853/is_200301/ai_n9191634* (January 2003).
11. "Latest Findings from the Congregational Project," *Congregations.Info: www.congregations.info/facts.html* (referenced September 22, 2005).
12. Thomas T. Huang, "The Diversity Gap," *Poynter Online: www.poynter. org/column.asp?id=58&aid=37934* (posted June 16, 2003).

Letter 4: Stonewashed Churches

1. Andrew Walsh, "Church, Lies, and Polling Data," *Religion in the News: www.trincoll.edu/depts/csrpl/RIN%20Vol.1No.2/church_lies_polling.htm* (accessed October 4, 2005).
2. "Betty Ford, A First Lady Who Tells It Like It Is," U.S.News.Com: *www.us news.com/usnews/doubleissue/heroes/ford/htm* (accessed October 3, 2005).
3. Sam Vincent Meddis, "The Web's Unexpected Political Clout," *USA Today: www.usatoday.com/tech/columnist/ccb0914.htm* (September 14, 1998).
4. "Talk Shows," *The Museum of Broadcast Communications: www.museum.tv/ archives/etv/T/htmlT/talkshows/talkshows.htm* (accessed October 3, 2005).
5. "Jerry Springer," *Wikipedia: en.wikipedia.org/wiki/Jerry_Springer* (accessed October 3, 2005).

6. Margaret Feinberg, "Seven Tactics That Will Never Work in Reaching a Twentysomething," *Church Planting Village: www.churchplantingvillage.net/site/c.iiJTKZPEJpH/b.992715/apps/s/content.asp?ct=1112829* (accessed October 3, 2005).

7. Andy Crouch, "Stonewashed Worship," *Christianity Today*, February 2005, 82.

Letter 5: Sketches in Progress

1. Margaret Feinberg, "The Emerging Church: An Interview with Dan Kimball," *Church Planting Village: www.churchplantingvillage.net/site/c.iiJTKZPEJpH/b.992715/apps/s/content.asp?ct=1183869* (accessed October 1, 2005).

2. Dean R. Hoge and Jacqueline E. Wenger, "Experiences of Protestant Ministers Who Left Local Church Ministry," *Pulpit and Pew Project of Duke University: www.pulpitandpew.duke.edu/Hoge.pdf* (presented October 25, 2003).

3. "Denominations Represented," *World Christian Database: www.worldchristiandatabase.org/wcd/about/denominationlist.asp* (posted in 2004).

4. "Spirituality Encountered More Effectively Outside Institutional Church," *Ekklesia: www.ekklesia.co.uk* (posted May 13, 2004).

5. Wolfgang Simpson, *Houses That Change the World* (Waynesboro, Ga.: Paternoster, 2001), 2.

6. Herb Drake, "House Church Turns 21 (Months That Is)," *House Church Central: www.hccentral.com/magazine/twenty.html* (October 1998).

7. "Registry of House Churches," *House Churches: www.housechurch.org/registry/index.html* (accessed October 1, 2005).

8. Cathy Lynn Grossman, "A New Generation Spreads the Word," *USA Today:www.usatoday.com/life/lifestyle/2004–06–23-christian-mag_x.htm* (posted June 23, 2004).

9. D. A. Carson, *Becoming Conversant with the Emerging Church* (Grand Rapids, Mich.: Zondervan, 2005), 234.

Letter 9: The Best Dirt I've Ever Eaten

1. "Theodore Roosevelt Association," *Man in the Arena: www.theodoreroosevelt.org/life/quotes.htm* (accessed December 9, 2005).

Letter 10: An Idea from a Guy Named Jesus

1. George Eldon Ladd, *A Theology of the New Testament* (Grand Rapids, Mich.: Eerdmans, 2000), 31.

Letter 12: Church at Home, Church on the Road

1. Glenn Tinder, *Political Thinking* (Boston: Little, Brown, 1974), 3.

2. Andy Stanley, *Visioneering* (Sisters, Ore.: Multnomah, 1999), 17.
3. N. T. Wright, *The Challenge of Jesus* (Downers Grove, Ill.: InterVarsity Press, 1999), 31.
4. Erwin McManus, *The Church in the Emerging Culture* (El Cajon, Calif.: Emergent

Letter 13: How Can We Go On Living?

1. Richard Foster, *Prayer: Finding the Heart's True Home* (New York: Harper Collins, 1964), 7–8.
2. N. T. Wright, *The Challenge of Jesus* (Downers Grove, Ill.: InterVarsity Press, 1999), 182.

Letter 14: Love Letters

1. Bill Hybels, *Courageous Leadership* (Grand Rapids, Mich.: Zondervan), 35.

We want to hear from you. Please send your comments about this book to us in care of zreview@zondervan.com. Thank you.

GRAND RAPIDS, MICHIGAN 49530 USA

ZONDERVAN.COM/
AUTHOR**TRACKER**